DEVELOPING
MULTI-MEDIA
LIBRARIES

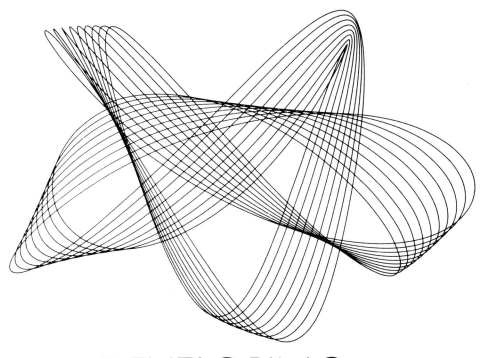

DEVELOPING
MULTI-MEDIA
LIBRARIES

Hicks, & Tillin
Warren B.

R. R. BOWKER COMPANY, New York & London

Published by R. R. Bowker Co. (A XEROX COMPANY)
1180 Ave. of the Americas, New York, N.Y. 10036

Standard Book Number: 8352-0265-8
Library of Congress Catalog Card Number: 72-112397

Printed and bound in the United States of America.

*The authors dedicate this volume to their
respective families, who through their
patience, intelligent understanding, and
technical assistance, demonstrated the
principle of INVOLVEMENT NOW in action.*

Contents

Illustrations

FIGURES

FORMS

TABLES

CATALOG CARDS

Sample catalog and circulation cards
for the various media will be found
following page 97.

Introduction

Lend me the stone strength of the past and I will lend you
The wings of the future, for I have them.
Robinson Jeffers

Today's librarians are aware that changes are occurring. Library, educational, audiovisual, and technical literature repeatedly inundates us with the causes and effects of technological advances and the knowledge explosion. In the midst of all this bombardment we may be losing sight of our basic library function, either clinging to out-moded concepts or promoting technology per se. With appropriate labels we have envisaged libraries of the future, sophisticated both in mechanical know-how and knowledge dissemination. Yet we must recognize that the library of today remains our ongoing responsibility. Whatever the type of library—public, county, school, special or academic—our obligation is to continuously up-date our service to reach an ever-widening circle of patrons. We must, therefore, provide resources in all those media that will best establish communication with every potential library patron.

This book presents the concept of the modern library as a comprehensive resource center. The philosophy and objectives of the center are clarified, and desirable practices in the selection and acquisition of nonbook or audiovisual materials—interchangeably defined as those materials that communicate primarily through aural and visual stimuli—are recommended, along with information pertinent to facilitating these tasks. Their organization in general is discussed, with emphasis on the necessity for basic decisions and policies. Cataloging and physical processing are treated in particular, demonstrating that accepted library practices can be flexible enough to allow adaptation for both the individual library and its specific clientele. Realistic methods of handling the many different kinds of nonbook materials are demonstrated by treating each type separately. Many easy-to-follow cataloging examples are presented; and, consistent with established library routine, practical information is provided on selection, acquisition, physical processing, storage, and equipment. Work-flow charts are included to present a graphic demonstration of efficient procedures.

Since school libraries have at present made the greatest strides in establishing resource centers for instructional materials, references are frequently made to practices used in educational facilities. The same process and procedures, however, would allow a library of any type or size to evolve into a resource center.

Librarians who are faced with the immediate task of integrating audiovisuals into existing book collections are seeking solutions to the technical problems generated by the uniqueness and variety of format of these materials. The intent of this book is to assist them by suggesting standardized procedures that show how the best elements of the traditional can be adapted to encompass continuous change. These practical, uncomplicated routines, while demanding the minimum expense in time and material, produce the organization which promotes maximum use of all resources, and frees those who are trained in librarianship to continue their most important function: working with the individual.

This book was written primarily for those librarians already familiar with standard library techniques. The degree to which the reader will benefit from the following text will depend upon his comprehension of acquisition, cataloging, and circulation of traditional printed library materials. No attempt has been made to present a treatise on how to classify, assign subject headings, or accomplish descriptive cataloging. This knowledge is the foundation on which the procedures for organizing nonbook materials are built. In addition, it is hoped that students currently in library education, who will soon be administering modern resource libraries, will find this text a helpful tool for expanding their basic preparation.

The authors wish to express their thanks to the many librarians, audiovisual specialists, and technology experts with whom they discussed the subjects treated in the following pages. Their identification of problems and constructive suggestions were major contributions in the writing of this book.

DEVELOPING MULTI-MEDIA LIBRARIES

PART I
AN OVERVIEW

1

THE CONCEPT OF MULTI-MEDIA LIBRARIES

THE FUNCTION AND THE EVOLUTIONARY PROCESS

Much has been said and much will continue to be said about the separate and combined world forces presently affecting libraries of every type. The impact of the computer has been described, the growth of knowledge and the flood of information statistically substantiated. Ideological and material changes have played their part, as have the possibly overwhelming demands that can be made on libraries by an ever-increasing population seeking new fields of employment, specialized skills, creative expression, and meaningful use of longer hours of lesiure. The consequences to libraries of swelling enrollments in higher education and the extension downward of public education to three-year-olds have been estimated. Nor have the revolutionary ideas of youth lacked effect.

It is only natural that the library respond to these changes. Its very existence has always rested on the premise that it functions as a community agency reflecting the entire society of which it is a part. To contribute to the total of man's life is the essence of library service, and this contribution can be accomplished by helping all people understand why revolutionary changes are occurring. The library practices this continuous guidance both by providing a record of man's cumulated knowledge and by ensuring that this record is communicated to each individual.

This concept must be fully understood by those responsible for libraries *before* they attempt to meet the challenge of change. Those who try to proceed without recognizing why they are involved are compounding their problems; those who see that they are really continuing the evolution of library processes discover that their problems are minimal. They create those practical methods which, while meeting the demands of the present, are at the same time, still flexible enough to build the bridge to the future. There is no need, then, to postpone action in carrying out that program that assists the individual in broadening his experience, deepening his aesthetic appreciation, and continuing his learning.

WHAT'S IN A NAME?

The simplest indicator of the changes we have been discussing is the rapid succession of names which have been applied in recent years to the institution traditionally known as "the library." No sooner has one label been proposed, explained, and applied than another version appears on the scene. But the names themselves are really not of any great importance. What is significant is that they are evidence of a concerted effort to redefine the function of the library. They signify repeated attempts to clarify that function for professional library personnel, and to promote full awareness of it among the general public.

Because of its support of instructional programs, the school library has been the recipient of the majority of the new terms. More closely geared to multi-media teaching and learning aids than are other types of libraries, its continuous reflection of the flux in educational philosophy and methods of instruction has made it the primary exponent of innovation. Unfortunately, this innovative spirit has produced a multitude of new terms that are all too often confusing in their similarity, although each is intended as an indication of a different emphasis in service.

The instructional materials center (IMC), and the educational media center (EMC) are conceptually parallel. Both developed from efforts to merge audiovisual services to classroom teachers with media services to individual students. The IMC came first. Initially simply called the audiovisual department or center, it was developed to support group instruction with different kinds of media. Its basic function was furnishing materials to faculty for teaching groups of students; service to the individual student was not included. As materials and equipment were developed for individual use, this latter service came into being, and the instructional materials center became the educational media center. The term "educational" was used instead of "instructional" to signify service to both teachers and students for teaching and learning. However, the EMC continued to stress service to the teacher, and direct service to individuals was still of secondary importance.

The *learning* center is based on the concept that the library is a place where learning *occurs*, rather than one in which learning materials are stored: its function is to promote learning by making both materials and services available to the student. Stress is laid on the moving of information to the student, not on the collecting of information. The role of the teacher changes from teaching to managing learning so that the student learns how to gain knowledge. The emphasis is on a one-to-one student-teacher relationship, on determining how a particular student learns and how services can best be utilized to facilitate his learning. By carrying out this concept to its fullest extent the place of learning becomes the entire school or college. Thus it is sometimes referred to as the library-college or library-school. Full acceptance of this idea requires drastic changes in traditional teaching methods and teacher training, and as of now it has not developed to an operational state.

Media center is the term used in the *Standards for School Media Programs* to designate "a learning center in a school where a full range of print and audiovisual media, necessary equipment, and services from media specialists are accessible to students and teachers."[1] The intent of the *Standards* is to provide a definition comprehensive enough to encompass all the services, facilities and resources now available to both students and teachers in school libraries—variously described as instructional materials centers, learning resource centers, library media centers— and in audiovisual departments—often referred to as communications centers, audiovisual centers, or instructional media centers. With a single administrative organization and a staff of competent specialists, the media center program presents a unified approach involving all types of media. The basic concept is service to the individual, which carries on and enlarges the tradition of individual- ized service with books.

It is unrealistic, however, to assume that the changing concepts expressed in these terms are limited to educational facilities. The terms already discussed— as well as others such as information, documentation, referral, and resource materials centers—can be applied to any kind of library. The same ideas, in varying stages of development, are found in the standards issued for every type of library. So in the pages that follow, the authors have chosen to perpetuate the use of the term library, thus retaining the connotation of individualized service which the term has carried for so long. At the same time, it has been combined with various adjectives—multi-media, modern—to indicate the diversity of its new responsibili- ties. The term "resource center" also appears, denoting not only the material, but also the human resources available in the library, for it must not be forgotten that the key to the application of these new concepts lies with the librarian, and nowhere else.

THE PATTERN

The modern library can rapidly become a reality when it is based on practical planning. Naturally, the long-range plans for each library cannot be the same, for each must satisfy the demands of its own community. Within the framework of its own program each library should identify those plans which can be implemented immediately, and establish a feasible rate of progression for the accomplishment of the others. Demonstration of change is important, and per- formance can successfully begin without waiting for the entire stage to be set.

The resource center could contain five areas, each one specially designed to accommodate printed materials, audiovisual materials, materials production, tele- vision, and electronic data or computer processing. To be operational, it would not need all these areas, but certainly enough of them to at least furnish the patron access to knowledge in whatever form it is carried. Nor do these areas always have to be distinctly divided. In many instances the integration of print and nonprint resources is more beneficial for the user than is their separation, and viewing and listening facilities can be incorporated within the area traditionally reserved for books. Indeed, the growing prevalence of microforms and facsimile transmission systems, which are really different formats of the book itself, empha- size that flexibility in area use should be very closely examined.

Materials production (and space for it) is not essential in the first phase of

[1] American Library Association and the National Education Association. *Standards for School Media Programs*. Prepared by a Joint Committee of the American Association of School Librarians and the Department of Audiovisual Instruction (Chicago: A.L.A., 1969), p. xv.

multi-media resource building. It must, however, be included and progressively developed in the over-all plan. Commercial sources and/or products are often unable to meet specific patron needs, and locally produced materials are frequently more effective, both in their subject content and method of presentation. They are, therefore, highly significant in rounding out the resource collection to its fullest scope.

Special areas for group viewing of television are not always needed. By installing the necessary equipment, other areas, such as classrooms and auditoriums, may be utilized for this purpose. However, since the continuous improvement in video tape production has increased the potential of television as a resource for individual use, the library should provide both the space and the hardware needed for its individual viewing and its local production. The possibilities for dial-access systems should also be seriously considered here. By furnishing this service the library gives each person unlimited, easy access to its collection of video and audio tapes, programmed materials, and other multi-media resources.

Electronic data or computer processing is rapidly becoming more and more important in the modern library. Automation of many of the repetitive routines in acquisition, cataloging, and circulation should free the librarian for more per-

FIGURE 1. DIAL ACCESS SYSTEMS. *Dial access systems furnish the library patron easy access to the library's collection of audio tapes.* (Photograph courtesy of Chabot College Library, Hayward, California.)

sonal service to the clientele. The value of the computer for the storage and retrieval of information also appears limitless. With the computer, local, regional, or even national communications networks can be connected to instantly tap the widest possible knowledge reservoirs, and the patron's search for immediate enlightenment need no longer be limited by the availability of resources in his own library. While the use of computers is not a current possibility for many resource centers, librarians should be aware of its rapidly increasing feasibility and plan for its future inclusion.

FIGURE 2. AUTOMATION IN THE LIBRARY. *Automation of many of the repetitive routines in acquisition, cataloging and circulation should free the librarian for more personal service to the patron. Here, an IBM 2260 is being used as an input device.* (Photograph courtesy of International Business Machines Corporation.)

The organizational pattern fashioned to administer the operational areas of the multi-media library will vary considerably with local conditions. The major objectives of the institution or community that it serves, the previously established administrative responsibilities, and the size and age of the physical facilities will all cause structural differences in administration. Fundamentally, however, there are two basic approaches in charting administration, centralization and decentralization. The former places all operational units under a single authority; the latter separates the authority for single units or a combination of units. Wherever possible, the administrational organization should follow the centralized pattern, as it has consistently demonstrated advantages which generate improvements in library services. The ability of single authority to adapt quickly to change and the close interrelationships among resources, facilities, equipment and staff all create efficiency and economy from which the patron benefits. Centralization also promotes the intelligent coordination of all activities in an integrated program which usually best satisfies the demands of the various library publics. Where existing arrangements dictate the decentralization of administration, the separate authorities must work very closely together to minimize needless duplication,

FIGURE 3. MICROFILM READER-PRINTER. *The growing use of microfilm is facilitated by the 35mm cartridge microfilm reader-printer with the coin-operated printing feature.* (Photograph courtesy of Chabot College Library, Hayward, California.)

excessive expense, wide dispersal of materials, and non-related operational units.

In the last analysis, the success of the modern library program depends not so much upon the degree of simplicity or sophistication of the spatial, technical and organizational array, as upon the enthusiasm, knowledge, and capabilities of the person who administers it. The truly creative librarian is the one who realizes the vast potential of the multi-media library for increased services and who, even though all of the conditions are not ideal, initiates immediate action. He applies his specialized training to enriching the existng collection with audiovisual resources efficiently organized for unrestricted access. He uses his talents to guide the individual in the use of these materials, suggesting their differing values and relationships. Even though budgets and space may be inadequate, he assures continuous library service by bringing knowledge to his patrons in all of its various and changing forms.

BIBLIOGRAPHY

American Library Association and the National Education Association. *Standards for School Media Programs*. Prepared by a Joint Committee of the American Association of School Librarians and the Department of Audiovisual Instruction. Chicago: A.L.A., 1969.

American Library Association. American Association of School Librarians. *Standards for School Library Programs*. Chicago: A.L.A., 1960.

American Library Association. Association of College and Research Libraries. *ALA Standards for College Libraries*. Chicago: A.L.A., 1959.

American Library Association. Association of College and Research Libraries. *ALA Standards for Junior College Libraries*. Chicago: A.L.A., 1960.

American Library Association. Association of College and Research Libraries. Audio-Visual Committee. *Guidelines for Audio-Visual Services in Academic Libraries*. Chicago: A.L.A., 1968.

American Library Association. Standards Committee of the Public Library Association. *Minimum Standards for Public Library Systems, 1966*. Chicago: A.L.A., 1967.

Anderson, Herschel V. *Audiovisual Services in the Small Public Library*. Small Libraries Project #17. Chicago: A.L.A., 1969.

Asheim, Lester E. "Education and Manpower for Librarianship; First Steps Toward a Statement of Policy." *ALA Bulletin* 62, No. 9 (Oct. 1968): 1096–1106.

A-V Task Force Survey: Final Report. Special summary prepared for the Audio-Visual Committee, American Library Association. Pittsburgh: University of Pittsburgh Libraries, 1969.

Bricks and Mortarboards: A Report on College Planning and Building. New York: Educational Facilities Laboratories, 1964.

Brown, James W., and Kenneth D. Norberg. *Administering Educational Media.* New York: McGraw-Hill, 1965.

Brown, Robert M. "The Learning Center." *AV Communication Review* 16, No. 3 (Fall 1968): 294–331.

De Kieffer, Robert E. *Audiovisual Instruction.* New York: Center for Applied Research in Education, 1965.

Dupuy, Trevor N. *Ferment in College Libraries: The Impact of Information Technology.* A report to the trustees of the College of the Potomac. Washington, D.C.: Communication Service Corporation, 1968.

Ellsworth, Ralph E. *The School Library.* New York: Center for Applied Research in Education, 1965.

———— and Hobart D. Wagener. *The School Library: Facilities for Independent Study in the Secondary School.* New York: Educational Facilities Laboratories, 1963.

Ely, Donald P., ed. *"The Changing Role of the Audio-Visual Process in Education: A Definition and a Glossary of Related Terms." AV Commuication Review*, Special Supplement, No. 6, vol. 11 (1963).

Erickson, Carlton W. H. *Administering Instructional Media Programs.* New York: Macmillan, 1968.

————. *Fundamentals of Teaching with Audiovisual Technology.* New York: Macmillan, 1965.

"Four Steps to a Learning Center." *Instructor* 76, No. 10 (Jun.-Jul. 1967): 73–84.

Gambee, Budd L. *Non-Book Materials as Library Resources.* Chapel Hill, N.C.: Student Stores, University of North Carolina, 1967.

Gaver, Mary V. *Patterns of Development in Elementary School Libraries Today: A Five Year Report on Emerging Media Centers.* 3rd ed. Chicago: Encyclopaedia Britannica, 1969.

Gross, Ronald, and Judith Murphy. *Educational Change and Architectural Consequences: A Report on Facilities for Individualized Instruction.* New York: Educational Facilities Laboratories, 1968.

Lohrer, Alice, ed. *The School Library Materials Center.* Champaign, Ill.: Illini Union Bookstore, 1964.

A Multi-Media Approach to Learning; Report of Special Conference in Provo, Utah, Sponsored by the Knapp School Libraries Project. Chicago: American Association of School Librarians, 1968.

"Objectives and Standards for Special Libraries." In *The Bowker Annual of Library and Book Trade Information, 1965*, pp. 132–133. New York: Bowker, 1965.

"See How They Learn." *Today's Education* 58, No. 2 (Feb. 1969): 15–32.

Stone, Walter C., ed. "Library Uses of the New Media of Communication." *Library Trends* 16, No. 2 (Oct. 1967).

Trenholme, A. K. "The New National Standards for School Media Programs: A Great Step Forward." *Audiovisual Instruction* 13, No. 7 (Sept. 1968): 697–699.

Wood, Raymund F. "Do We Need a New Terminology for Librarianship?" *California Librarian* 29, No. 4 (Oct. 1968): 274–278.

2

MULTI-MEDIA RESOURCES EVALUATION

MATERIALS SELECTION POLICY

Experience has shown that a written statement of policy is basic in the selection
of library materials. The very formulation of a policy, accomplished coopera-
tively by all personnel who will be involved in selection, demands an in-depth
evaluation and clear rethinking of philosophy and objectives. Vague, general
and repetitious criteria are critically analyzed and restated as meaningful useable
guides. An officially approved policy provides support and free exercise of professional judgment to those responsible for selection. It serves as a source of
communication, a clarification of purpose, and an instrument for public relations
to the community in general.

Many libraries currently have a book selection policy which contains principles applicable to nonbook materials. However, to realistically cover all media
included in the collection of the resource center, revision and expansion of an
existing policy or adoption of a new one is essential. For both protection and
guidance the statement of policy governing selection must have the sanction of
the administration of the institution and of its official controlling body.

Perusal of officially adopted statements of other libraries will facilitate the
preparation of materials selection policies. These may be general or specific in
their coverage. As a rule, they clarify the philosophy and objectives of materials
selection and identify both the legal, official entity and the personnel responsible
for implementation. They may also list the various types of material involved as
well as general and specific criteria for evaluation. Criteria for special subject areas
such as sex, religion, narcotics, and political doctrines, may be stated in detail. In
addition, procedures for selection, for gift acceptance, and for handling questioned
materials are frequently included. Many policies also contain excerpts from such
supporting publications as the American Library Association's *Library Bill of
Rights*, the American Association of School Librarians' *School Library Bill
of Rights*, President Eisenhower's statement on *The Freedom to Read*, and the
National Council of Teachers of English *Students' Right to Read*.

How general or specific the complete materials selection policy should be will be influenced by various local factors. Those responsible for the formulation of the policy will have to assess prevailing conditions in the area served, the temper of the community, the opinions found on the governing board, and previous policies and precedents. The important point is that an officially adopted policy exist. (See Bibliography at end of chapter for aids in materials selection policy preparation.)

SELECTION CRITERIA

Discriminating choice of audiovisual materials cannot be based on the traditional idea that they are nothing more than handmaidens to the book. They must be clearly and objectively viewed in their own right. Their merits must be evaluated, not in comparison to books and magazines, but in an assessment of their own specific contribution to satisfying the often unexpressed needs of the library public. This revised viewpoint recognizes the shortcomings of a library collection tailored generally to middle class suburbia; its awareness of current changes continuously emphasizes and aggressively seeks service to the individual, whatever may be his intellectual, social or economic situation.

FIGURE 4. NONBOOK MATERIALS AND BOOKS. *Nonbook materials are, in reality, complements to books.* (Photograph courtesy of the Oakland, California, Public Schools.)

These concepts reaffirm the importance of two familiar and accepted principles considered fundamental in the selection of all types of materials: a comprehensive knowledge of the populace and its desires, and an extensive fund of information on all kinds of resources. Without a knowledge of the people who will use the resources and a knowledge of the materials themselves any attempt to formulate criteria for selection will only lead to confusion.

Stated criteria are in themselves only operational guidelines. It should always be understood that any set of criteria must have the flexibility to permit common sense adaptations to both specific materials and particular situations. Rigidity in criteria and literalness in their interpretation can produce both frustration for the librarian and a collection lacking in those elements essential for communication with all individuals and groups. Relevancy, as determined by changing conditions and varying audiences, promotes communication, and as such, is of basic importance in selection.

When the customary evaluation criteria of authenticity, appropriateness, scope, interest, organization, special features, and physical characteristics are seen in the light of such factors as type of library and its desired goals, patron homoge-

FIGURE 5. AUDIOVISUAL MATERIALS IN USE IN A PUBLIC LIBRARY. (Photograph courtesy of the Livermore, California, Public Library.)

neity or heterogeneity, and availability of materials, their relative importance will vary. For example, acquisitions for a school library or media center collection are chosen from a point of view which emphasizes furtherance of stated learning objectives, relevancy to curriculum, stimulus or response as related to current teaching methods, and broadening of intellectual, emotional and creative experiences. Comparatively, the public library may wish to lay more stress on those items which encompass a broader spectrum and are less specific in their application.

Audiovisuals are judged by the previously mentioned criteria, which pertain to all materials, and also by technical quality. Esthetic standards relating to effective composition, proper focus, and cogent use of color, are applied to the visual image. Clarity and intelligibility, combined with pleasing tone elements, are required from the audio product. Where sound and picture are synthesized, sychronization is essential.

Characteristics that rate high or low on the quality scale are presented here in a positive form rather than in the traditional questioning manner. It is understood that all of them cannot be applied in every instance. Their suitability is determined, in part, by the sort of matter under consideration, e.g., fiction or nonfiction. Although such a list cannot be entirely comprehensive it suggests a ready reference instrument for facilitating the rapid identification of salient points in the selection process. Additional criteria, relevant to a *particular* kind of resource (e.g., maps), are treated in detail in the latter part of the book.

TABLE 1. CRITERIA FOR SELECTION OF NONBOOK MATERIALS

POINTS OF QUALITY	POINTS OF INFERIORITY
(Accept)	(Reject)

LOOK FOR
AUTHENTICITY

Accurate facts	Inaccurate facts
Facts impartially presented	Facts distorted by bias
Up-to-date information	Fake revised version: date only changed, no up-dating of contents
Other acceptable works of producer	Consistent rejection of other works of producer

APPROPRIATENESS

Vocabulary at user's level	Vocabulary too easy or difficult
Concepts at user's level	Concepts too easy or difficult
Useful data	Extraneous data
Media-subject correlation (e.g., art prints to art, specimens to science)	Media does not add to subject communication
Titles, captions, etc. related to subject	Titles, captions, etc. confuse subject concepts
Narration, dialogue, sound effects related to subject	Narration, dialogue, sound effects unrelated to subject
Individual and/or group use suitability	Limited individual and/or group use suitability

POINTS OF QUALITY	POINTS OF INFERIORITY
(Accept)	(Reject)

SCOPE

Full coverage as indicated	Gaps in coverage
Superior concept development by this means	Better concept development by other means
Content to satisfy demands for current subjects	Irrelevance to current topics

INTEREST

Relationship to user's experience	No relationship to user's cultural environment
Intellectual challenge	No intellectual challenge
Curiosity satisfaction	No satisfactory answers
Credibility	Implausibility
Imagination appeal	Prosaic presentation
Human appeal	Negative human values
Sensory appeal	No stimulation

ORGANIZATION

Logical development	Confused development; excessive repetition
Pertinence of all sequences	Unrelated sequences
Balance in use of narration and dialogue; music and sound effects; background elements	Ineffective or overpowering use of the same elements

TECHNICAL ASPECTS

Tone fidelity	Tone distortion
Clarity	Extraneous sounds, visuals too detailed
Intelligibility	Difficulty in following image and/or sound
In-focus pictures	Fuzzy out-of-focus pictures
True size relationships	Unreal size relationships
Unified composition	Confused composition
Effective color use	Color is less effective than black and white
Complete synchronization of sound and image	Uneven synchronization of sound and image

SPECIAL FEATURES

Descriptive notes, teachers and/or users guide	Absence of useful notes, guides
Pertinent accompanying material	Unrelated materials packaged together

PHYSICAL CHARACTERISTICS

Ease in handling, for user, for storage	Difficulty in handling
Minimum instruction for individual use	Special training requirements for use
Attractive packaging	Unattractive packaging
Durability	Flimsy construction
Ease of repair	Difficulty in repairing damage

POINTS OF QUALITY	POINTS OF INFERIORITY
(Accept)	(Reject)

LIBRARY POTENTIAL

Relevancy that promotes communication	No furthering of communication
Flexibility for many effective uses	Features which limit use

SELECTION AIDS

Recommendation in evaluation sources	Rejection in evaluation sources

COST

Conformity to budget	Too costly for budget
No less expense for satisfactory substitutes	Satisfactory substitutes cheaper
Inexpensive or already purchased equipment	Expensive equipment needed
Economy if purchased	Greater expense to rent
Average supplemental costs for replacement, repair, physical processing, storage	Too expensive to replace, repair, process for use

MATERIALS SPECTRUM

Together with its traditional collections of books and periodicals, the modern library provides a critically selected collection of audiovisual materials. The majority of them require special equipment for reproduction, and the number and kinds of these materials continue to increase, so the librarian will have a vast array from which to choose. It is essential, therefore, to identify the peculiar benefit inherent in each type, and to understand especially why and how it can be used by the individual in the library. This perception is expedited by grouping together materials that are related because they achieve communication through similar means. The importance of the purpose of the medium, rather than the physical properties of the material, is emphasized by division into the following broad categories:

STILL-PROJECTION MATERIALS Filmstrips, microforms, slides, transparencies; projected opaque materials. Those visuals which are projected without motion are referred to as still-projection materials. Their attention-focusing value for group viewing has long been accepted. For individual viewing they have additional merit. Since comprehension is not dependent on motion, each patron can control the speed of the presentation, and modern still-projection equipment permits him to do this both in the library *and* in his own home. He can grasp concepts more rapidly because the sequential order of still-projected materials, proceeding from the known to the unknown, enables him to visualize the developmental process. At the same time he can manipulate that order to accommodate his own mode of understanding.

The great range of subject matter covered by still-projected materials adds to their value. The number and types of filmstrips available seem to be infinite. With a local production facility as part of the modern library, the number and scope of slides and transparencies is limited only by the needs and the budget. These resources, with their wide content span and flexibility for individual use, may often be the means of reaching the non-readers who would otherwise not frequent the library.

MOTION-PROJECTION MATERIALS 16mm and 8mm films, kinescopes, video tapes. Motion-projection materials consist of a series of still pictures shown in rapid succession so that the viewer has an illusion of motion. They may be silent or carry their own sound track. Their library potential is based upon their ability to substitute for demonstrations or for the direct experience itself. Through these media it is possible to go back in history, visit other countries, see an experiment in slow motion, or observe changes in nature which cannot be seen by the human eye. This creates interest and extends the range of human experience.

The 16mm motion picture film is generally considered a group device. As a permanent part of the resource collection it is restricted by its high cost, thereby

FIGURE 6. TRANSPARENCIES. *Transparencies, long used for group viewing, have definite advantages for individual use as well.* (Photograph courtesy of Chabot College Library, Hayward, California.)

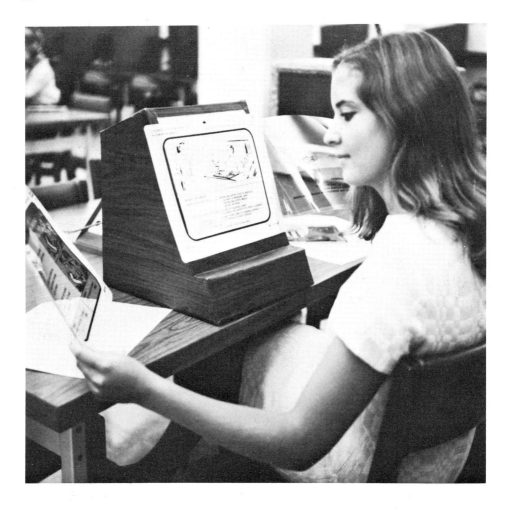

FIGURE 7. MOTION PROJECTION MATERIALS. *Motion projection materials create interest and extend the range of human experience.* (Photograph courtesy of the Oakland, California, Public Schools.)

reducing what any single library can provide to immediately fill a request. However, patron's needs could be served on a delayed basis by developing procedures to obtain a wealth of 16mm films from many rental and loan sources. With the advancement of technology and clearance under copyright laws, films could be projected over television from a central film depository directly to a patron in a local library. With the emphasis changing in educational instruction from group-centered methods to those involving independent study, the concept of the individual utilization of the 16mm film has emerged. And it has been strengthened by the recent provision of rear projection equipment, which makes individual viewing in a library situation entirely feasible.

For the library, one of the most important developments in motion projection is the 8mm loop, often called the single-concept film. Produced in a cartridge, it features a short running time; and it can be projected in a well-lighted room

FIGURE 8. 16MM REAR PROJECTION EQUIPMENT. *The recent development of 16mm rear projection equipment has resulted in increased individual use
of 16mm films in the library.* (Photograph courtesy of Viewlex, Inc.)

through rear projection equipment. The individual can easily operate the equipment and repeat the film loop as often as needed, without being concerned with
threading or rewinding the film. Covering an ever-widening range of subjects, the
8mm film is relatively inexpensive, and is now available either as a silent or sound
presentation. With continued improvement in sound synchronization and increased production of longer-running films treating more than one subject, it may
become a very adequate substitute for the more costly 16mm film. All these evident advantages have demonstrated that motion-projection materials can successfully serve the individual in the library.

Television can be a vital force in extending the availability of motion-projection resources. Programs recorded in kinescope or video tape form can be reprojected when needed. By this means, the whole gamut of subjects covered by
television can become part of the library collection. And with the combination of
the video tape recorder and the closed circuit system, the library can provide this
wide variety of information immediately upon demand. It is entirely feasible that,
in the very near future, it will be common practice to check out a video tape from
the library for viewing on home television sets.

Production of video recordings and equipment for home use has already
begun. Electronic Video Recording (EVR) is a two-channel audiovisual tape in a
special 7-inch cartridge that can be played on an attachment to a TV set. It provides up to fifty-two minutes of programming. The cartridge is self-loading and
the film-like tape is sprocketless and encased in a cushion of air to reduce friction

FIGURE 9. VIDEO TAPE EQUIPMENT IN THE LIBRARY. *Programs re-corded on video tape can be reprojected, when needed by the library patron.* (Photograph courtesy of Chabot College Library, Hayward, California.)

and damage. Like the 8mm cartridge film it feeds directly from cartridge to player and back again, remaining clean and protected from wear and tear. The player mechanism is attached to any TV set by placing a clamp on the antenna terminals. Eventually, this playback unit may become a built-in feature of every television receiver. As more films are converted to EVR format and new educational and recreational programs are produced as electronic video recordings, the individual will be able to make his own selection and schedule his viewing to his convenience at home.

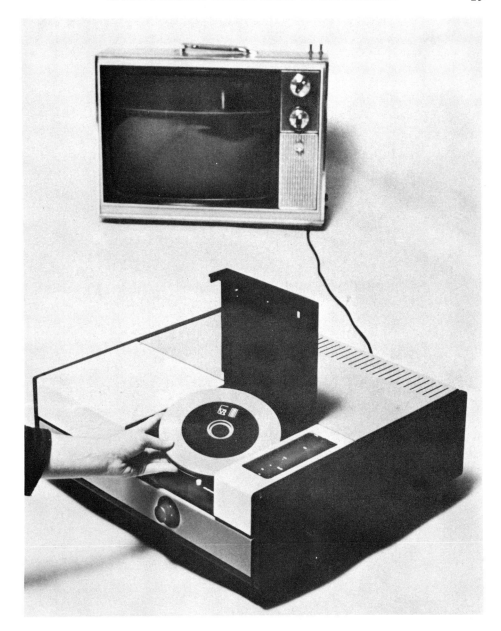

FIGURE 10. ELECTRONIC VIDEO RECORDING EQUIPMENT. *With such equipment as the CBS electronic video recording, it would be possible for the library to make material available for viewing on home television sets.* (Photograph courtesy of Columbia Broadcasting System, Inc.)

AUDIO MATERIALS Disc and tape recordings. The reproduction of sound recorded on discs and tapes is now an indispensable part of our educational and recreational activities. Through these recordings the listener can participate in experiences ranging from the starkly realistic to the purely imaginative.

Disc recordings have a tremendous library potential because of the variety and quantity of material they offer. The range is wide, from stories for pre-schoolers to sophisticated drama, opera, and poetry reading for adults. The works of Shakespeare, speeches of Kennedy, world-wide folk music, and exotic languages such as Swahili and Esperanto have all been recorded. Record players are now considered an essential part of home furnishings, and the manufacturing technique of producing phonograph records in mass duplication has tended to keep their cost within reasonable limits. However, they can be easily damaged and rapidly worn out. Nor can they be repaired, or duplicated in their same form in a non-commercial production center.

Tapes are a medium parallel to discs, with features especially advantageous for library service. They wear much longer, are more resistant to change, and can be produced locally with simple equipment. The conventional reel-to-reel type is now being challenged by cassette tapes and recorders that permit much wider individualized library use. They are relatively inexpensive, compact and lightweight. Since the cassette completely encloses the tape and snaps into the correct position for playback, no threading skills are required from the listener, the danger of erasure is minimized, and the impairment incidence is lowered.

Individual access to audio tapes in the library can also be provided through an automatic system. The patron uses a telephone-type dial to request his selection, and it is automatically transmitted to him. Computer-directed remote access sys-

FIGURE 11. TAPES AND THE EAR. *Tape recordings present subject coverage so broad that they may do for the ear what the printed page has done for the eye.* (Photograph courtesy of 3M/Wollensak.)

tems will allow random access to all of the tapes in a library, and even to those of other libraries.

Because of their tremendous versatility and ability to satisfy a multitude of individual differences, tape recordings must be considered essential to the library resource collection.

FLAT GRAPHIC MATERIALS   Art and study prints, charts, maps, flash cards, pictures. Although often loosely referred to as "pictures," the scope of graphic materials is far wider than this term denotes. Actually, they include any surface representation which visualizes concrete subjects and abstract ideas. Since their form is so varied and their content so extensive, their treatment is simplified by separating them into several different groups. These divisions may be based on the subject they illustrate, on their graphic technique, and on their intended use.

Art prints are subject based, since they are limited to reproductions of works of art only. Study prints and flash cards are so designated to accentuate their contribution to instructional methods. Charts summarize real and abstract concepts in both the humanities and the sciences through diagrammatic, tabular and pictorial means. Maps are usually regarded primarily as place media but their scope is not limited to showing geographic location. By employing combinations of diverse symbols they also visualize many other important topics such as ethnic relationships, physical, social and economic conditions, and historical, artistic and literary development. Pictures, for library classification purposes, comprise all those miscellaneous forms of illustration which do not specifically identify with any other category. Reproductions of documents, photographs, post cards, posters, and cartoons are all contained in this group.

The high potential of graphics for individual study dictates their inclusion in the resource center. There is little difficulty in acquiring them, for they exist in quantity and, on the average, are low in price. Their use requires no special equipment either in or out of the library, and each person is free to regulate his own perusal time. In many instances they may substitute for other, less easily obtained material, because their current sophisticated techniques of illustration can evoke uniquely personal emotional and intellectual experiences. At the same time, graphic material can combine admirably with other media to complete a multi-sensory impact.

THREE-DIMENSIONAL MATERIALS   Dioramas, games, globes, kits, mock-ups, models, realia, specimens. Three-dimensional materials may consist of real objects, their facsimiles, or, where it is impossible to present the actual thing, reproductions scaled down to practical size or fabricated to emphasize functional characteristics. For every person they can supply a firsthand experience otherwise unobtainable, providing him with the opportunity to extend his horizons through all his senses. The library potential of three-dimensional resources is further enhanced by their subject versatility and suitability for patrons of all ages and intelligence levels. In addition, their inherent interest and ability to stimulate frequently triggers motivation which cannot be accomplished through other devices.

PROGRAMMED MATERIALS   Programmed materials are both printed and nonprinted matter that has been designed specifically to help the individual learn. They enable him to study carefully structured lessons that he progressively masters at his own pace. Some programs appear as films, filmstrips, books, or combinations of these and other forms. The presentation of other programs requires a teaching machine, either a simple user-operated device or computer-assisted equipment.

Possible uses of programmed material in the library are limitless. While it is intended as an instructional aid it should not be restricted to libraries serving educational institutions. It has great potential in public libraries for meeting informational and educational needs. For enrichment and basic information short programs with limited specific objectives would be extremely popular. Many people who are self-motivated and desire to continue their own education could utilize these resources of the public library in their learning process. Special libraries with demands in particular subjects and skills can also use programmed materials to satisfy individual instructional needs. With the increasing diversity of subjects programmed and the development of computer and microform technology it will be entirely possible for all libraries to accommodate many more individual differences in learning.

An essential adjunct to audiovisual resources is the equipment necessary for their presentation. Since the benefit derived from nonbook materials may frequently depend on the listening and viewing equipment available, it is advisable to consider selection and organization of the equipment concurrently with that of the materials themselves.

Vertical file materials are an additional source of useful and current information which should be a part of the library's resources. Here are found a variety of miscellaneous items of varying format that communicate via the printed word and through visual imagery. They will contribute only frustration to the searcher unless they are selectively chosen and well arranged for easy accessibility.

BIBLIOGRAPHY

* Those entries marked with an asterisk will be found to be particularly useful in materials selection policy preparation.

*American Library Association. *Freedom in Inquiry; Supporting the Library Bill of Rights.* Proceedings of the Conference on Intellectual Freedom, January 23–24, 1965. Chicago: A.L.A., 1965.

*――――. American Association of School Librarians. *Policies and Procedures for Selection of School Library Materials.* Chicago: A.L.A., 1961.

*――――. American Association of School Librarians. *Selecting Materials for School Libraries; Guidelines and Selection Sources to Insure Quality Collections.* Chicago: A.L.A., 1965.

――――― and the National Education Association. *Standards for School Media Programs.* Prepared by a Joint Committee of the American Association of School Librarians and the Department of Audiovisual Instruction. Chicago: A.L.A., 1969.

Brown, James W., and Richard B. Lewis. *A-V Instruction: Media and Methods.* 3rd ed. New York: McGraw-Hill, 1969.

Bruner, Bernice. "Public Libraries Utilize Non-Book Activities and Material in Work with Children." *Library Trends* 12 (July 1963): 71–83.

*California Association of School Librarians. *Instructional Materials: Selection Policies and Procedures.* P.O. Box 1277, Burlingame, Calif.: CASL Publications, 1965.

Cochran, Lida M. "Four Significant Media Projects of 1967–1968." *Audiovisual Instruction* 13 (June–July 1968): 578–583.

Cory, Patricia B. "Public Library Film Services from Start till Now." *Film News* 23 (June–July 1966): 5–6.

Gaver, Mary V., and Marian Scott. *Evaluating Library Resources for Elementary School Libraries*. East Brunswick, N.J.: SSH Press, 1962.

Gross, Elizabeth H. *Public Library Service to Children*. Dobbs Ferry, N.Y.: Oceana Publications, 1967.

Guss, Carolyn. "Evaluating and Selecting Instructional Materials." In *A Multi-Media Approach to Learning*. Chicago: A.L.A., 1968.

Kilpatrick, Elizabeth G. "Do We Need New Directions?" *Top of the News* 24 (June 1968): 399–406.

Logasa, Hannah. *Book Selection Handbook for Elementary and Secondary School*. Boston: F. W. Faxon, 1953.

Rufsvold, Margaret I. *Audio-Visual School Library Service: A Handbook for Librarians*. Chicago: A.L.A., 1949.

Shores, Louis. *Instructional Materials: An Introduction for Teachers*. New York: Ronald Press, 1960.

Tosti, Donald T., and John R. Ball. "A Behavioral Approach to Instructional Design and Media Selection." *AV Communication Review* 17 (Spring 1969): 5–25.

3

SELECTION OF
MULTI-MEDIA RESOURCES

ASSISTANCE IN CHOOSING

As educational and sociological progress occurs, both technical and ideational changes ensue in the resources available, in ever increasing quantity and variety. Recognition of the rapidity of these innovations is evidenced by the recommendation that the national *Standards for School Media Programs* be reviewed every two years. Both the obligation to keep up to date and the consideration of an expanding volume of materials could become overwhelming, were it not for the use of certain means which help in the selection process.

At the present time, although advances are being made, aids to selection in the media field are inferior in number, and often in quality to those that deal only with books. The most prevalent assistance is in the choosing of instructional materials for the school media center. This is a direct result of the interest of educators who are alert to the importance of varied media in the individual's learning process. The determination to make available to students, teachers, and librarians, the best educational ideas, innovations, and resources, has recently been translated into action by a grant from the Bureau of Research of the U.S. Office of Education to the National Book Committee. The purpose of this funding is to improve educational media selection centers. The project will be carried out in four phases over a 7½-year period. When standards and guidelines have been formulated, the ultimate aim is to establish model or demonstration selection centers that will house an extensive range of professionally chosen print and nonprint materials. These collections will be utilized to train and assist librarians and teachers in evaluating, selecting, and using materials with children of differing needs and backgrounds. A coordinated publication and film communications network will disseminate information. Even though projects such as these, and other media selection tools refer specifically to the school situation, their use need not be this limited. With the necessary adaptations all types of libraries will profit from them.

AID THROUGH INVOLVEMENT

Depending upon the type of library and the particular clientele for which it exists, the concept of involvement is referred to under various labels. Partnership, participation, cooperation, working combination, these are some of the currently popular terms. Whatever it may be called, it re-emphasizes the necessity for constant and close communication between library and patrons, whether they be teachers, students, faculty members, or citizens of the community. Such close cooperation assists in establishing the library as a service rather than storage agency.

With regard to selection, involvement specifically helps to implement two fundamental principles, knowledge of the people, and knowledge of materials. On the one hand, continuous information supplied both by students and citizens, and those working with them, assists the librarian in determining the types of materials that best satisfy the demand. On the other hand, even though subject specialists are now being added to the staffs of some large and academic libraries, those responsible for selection could not possibly be expert in every subject field. Thus, suggestions from non-library subject specialists are a valuable aid in ensuring the best acquisitions in many specialized areas.

AID THROUGH PREVIEW AND AUDITION

Although personal reviewing, previewing, and auditioning have long been considered the ideal methods of selection, their feasibility is limited by several factors. Chief among these is the increasing volume of resources now being produced and the consequent decreasing amount of time available for individualized inspection. The purchase of books based on recommendations appearing in several well-known authoritative review sources, rather than on selectors' perusals, is now accepted practice. Valuable time is reserved for a closer look at those publications that show no review consensus, or that have not been reviewed, or that pertain to a specialized subject area or distinctive local need. This same technique could be successfully applied in nonbook selection. However, since evaluative reviews of multi-media resources are far from comprehensive, previewing and auditioning remain the principal source of information.

Certain logistical problems are inherent in previewing and auditioning. They necessitate the acquisition, setting-up, and operation of adequate equipment, in a facility which can supply room darkening and suitable acoustics. Rather than taking the material with him and evaluating it at his convenience, the selector may have to go to a previewing center, and often at definitely scheduled dates.

The procurement and return of materials for preview demands a systematized organization. According to the type of material, and the practice of each individual producer, the preview loan period may be short or long term, varying anywhere from ten to fifteen days to an entire academic year. Close coordination is often required to work out a schedule of preview sessions which are suitable to personnel and still coincide with various receiving and obligatory return dates. Since producers may differ on their terms and conditions for preview, these should be carefully checked before requests are placed. Return procedures must also be devised to minimize the time consumed in verifying identification and possible damage, and in packaging and mailing odd-sized cumbersome items. If materials are not available for preview, as may often occur, the library must decide whether acquisition should be made on the strength of the producer's recommendation or whether additional information or comparable items should be researched from other sources.

Since the previewing-auditioning process must operate within the framework of these several realistic limitations, its utilization should be guided by a flexible practical policy. Thus, in answer to the question: "Why preview and audition?", the most relevant reasons are:

> To determine the degree of library potential: the estimated fulfill-ment of known needs; the possibilities for use in a variety of different ways; the unique effectiveness in communicating, especially when compared to other available resources.
> To evaluate the medium itself, irrespective of its particular subject content.
> To judge the capacity for integration: with cultural, social and learning experiences of the clientele; with other materials for interrelated usage.
> To ascertain technical quality.
> To appraise subject content, its treatment and presentation, particularly in specialized areas.

Previewing-auditioning cannot be done by one person alone, even though his qualifications are of the highest. They demand a pooling of human resources, and reactions from varied personnel: those who are competent in over-all selection techniques, those who work closely with all population groups, those who are technical experts, and those who are subject specialists. Without a synthesis of their opinions there can be no guarantee of excellence in selection.

AID THROUGH REVIEWS

In the foregoing discussion of selection aids some of the benefits derived from reviews were indicated. In summary, this technique is valuable because:

> It minimizes unnecessary duplication where the reviewing source has an established reliable reputation.
> It maximizes efficient use of valuable professional time for: More comprehensive coverage of all materials; more discerning examination of those resources which lack adequate reviews; more service with the individual patron.
> It provides a broader basis of critical appraisal, furnishes technical and subject specialization expertise, lessens the logistical problems of previewing-auditioning, and increases the speed of acquisition.

Obviously, the utility of the review method varies with the quantity and quality of reviews available. As yet, the scope of media evaluations is still far from all-inclusive. This applies both to the number of resources appraised, and to the expressions of critical opinion on any one item. The lack of multiple reviews considerably narrows the spectrum of expert judgment on which to base selection.

In addition, the art of multi-media reviewing has not attained that state of sophistication which ensures superior quality. Since there are few guidelines, many supposedly evaluative reviews fail to analyze essential or unique facets. A good review should comment on those singular characteristics of the material which would otherwise have to be determined by previewing-auditioning, as discussed on the previous page.

The reliability and reputation of the reviewing source can be measured by criteria paralleling those used to evaluate book reviews. In media reviewing, however, knowledge of the evaluator's background becomes an important consideration. A wide divergence of opinion may appear in reviews written by those who are educated and experienced primarily in audiovisual technology, or in traditional librarianship, or in a happy combination of the two. As the current shortage of the last is alleviated, more and better reviewing of nonbook materials for all types of libraries can be expected.

In using reviews as a selection tool, a distinction should be made between those that are evaluative and those that are simply descriptive. Regular scanning of descriptive reviews is a quick and practical way to gain a broader acquaintance with existing materials and keep up with current releases. They report objectively on subject content and physical characteristics, and present correct bibliographical detail, which often minimizes further checking for acquisition and cataloging. They do not make critical or evaluative statements, although they sometimes offer suggestions for use. If properly used, this type of review can make the selection process more efficient: because it indicates which materials would not be pertinent, it automatically narrows the number of items that need previewing. In itself, however, it cannot be considered a valid basis of selection. The material it describes must be evaluated through preview or some means of testing.

Regular, dependable, evaluative book reviews, geared to different kinds of libraries and comprehensive in their subject coverage, can be relied upon for assistance in selection. As yet, however, critical appraisals of multi-media materials, suitable for different types of libraries and pertaining to all fields of knowledge, are still in their infancy. The majority of those available are specifically oriented to libraries involved in educational programs. Written from an "aid to instruction" point of view, they often tend to emphasize the potential for group rather than individual use. Reviewing in periodical literature has already established the pattern of treating the resources of each medium separately. Films (16mm and some 8mm), filmstrips, and recordings (disc and tape) receive paramount attention, with other media grouped together as miscellaneous offerings. Little attempt has been made to regularly present evaluative overviews of all the media that bear on any one subject. Such a subject approach would bring into clearer focus the purpose of the medium and the interrelationships among the various media. It would permit critical comparison to establish media potential since, in many content areas, certain information is better expressed through one kind of medium than through any other, e.g., seed pollination through motion pictures. In effect, it would ensure selection of the best resources to meet specific needs.

Selected subject cross-media resources are frequently included in magazine articles. These are very worthwhile, but because of their sporadic appearance, are difficult to keep track of and cannot be depended upon for continual information about new releases. Very often they take the form of an unannotated list that gives little indication of the specific values of the materials. The second edition of *Guides to Newer Educational Media* by Margaret I. Rufsvold and Carolyn Guss (Chicago: A.L.A., 1967) should be consulted for a comprehensive descriptive listing of where to obtain both descriptive and evaluative reviews. The sources selected here furnish only evaluative information on more than one type of material. They have been grouped so that a clearer picture of multi-media reviewing may be seen.

PERIODICALS

These serially feature evaluative reviews of new materials in more than one medium.

Audiovisual Instruction. Department of Audiovisual Instruction, National Education Association, 1201 16th St., N.W., Washington, D.C. 20036. Monthly. Membership (Nonmembers, $8).

Provides evaluative-descriptive reviews in its regular department, "Materials in Review." Its "Index of Audiovisual Reviews" and "Index of Audio Reviews" facilitate quick location of reviews in about twenty educational periodicals.

The Booklist (Formerly *The Booklist and Subscription Books Bulletin*) American Library Association, 50 E. Huron St., Chicago, Ill. 60611. Semi-monthly. $10.

Nonprint media reviewing began in the Sept. 1, 1969, issue with reviews of filmstrips and 8mm films. Transparencies, nonmusical recordings, and 16mm films will be added later. Evaluations are made by consultant groups selected nationwide from elementary and secondary school districts, colleges and universities, and public libraries. Only items recommended for purchase appear in *The Booklist*. Besides summarizing content, annotations point out specific audiences, age level, interest appeal, and possible uses. Information given includes complete bibliographic data, price, subject headings, and Library of Congress card number, if available.

Educational Product Report (Formerly, *EPIE Forum*). Educational Products Information Exchange (EPIE) Institute, 386 Park Ave. S., New York, N.Y. 10016. Monthly (October through June, with a special supplement in each of the nine issues). $35 (includes membership in the Institute).

The *Report* gathers, synthesizes, and disseminates opinions and technical analyses of educational products based on standard evaluation criteria. Producers, reviewers, laboratory testers, and users are all contributors. Each "Product Information Supplement" deals with a particular area, and priority in subject matter is determined by survey. The comprehensive, fact-filled coverage of the materials available on any one subject constitute an excellent basis for making critical comparisons. Initially the listings were descriptive. However, an increasing number of evaluative analyses of product classes are now being issued. To date, some of the materials reported on include: programmed instruction (kindergarten through 12th grade) in science, mathematics, social studies; elementary science kits; resources in secondary school mathematics, and in sex education; and materials for use with disadvantaged students.

Educational Screen and AV Guide. 434 South Wabash Ave., Chicago, Ill. 60605. Monthly. $4.

Motion pictures, filmstrips, and phonodiscs are regularly reviewed.

Film News: The Newsmagazine of Films, Filmstrips, Recordings, Educational TV. Film News Co., 250 W. 57 St., New York, N.Y. 10019. Bi-monthly. $5.

> Descriptive and evaluative annotations of films, filmstrips, and phonodiscs are regular features.

The Instructor. Instructor Publications, Inc., Instructor Park, Dansville, N.Y. 14437. Monthly. $7.

> Reviews of curriculum materials: films, filmstrips, kits, charts, and other related resources. Valuable for suggestions for use.

School Library Journal. R. R. Bowker Co., 1180 Ave. of the Americas, New York, N.Y. 10036. Monthly (September through May). $5.

> In addition to providing, in various issues, lists of selected recordings, films, and filmstrips to be used with children and young adults in public and school libraries, two regular *SLJ* departments—"Recordings" and "Screenings"—present monthly reviews of records, filmstrips, 16mm and 8mm films. Other media such as slides, transparencies, study prints and documentary packets are also included, under the heading "Media Mix."

> An additional service—*The Audiovisual Guide: A Multimedia Subject List*—was initiated in November, 1967, with regular semi-annual issues appearing every April and November. It is a comprehensive, non-evaluative presentation of current media, arranged by subject, including filmstrips, 8 and 16mm films, disc recordings, transparencies, slides, tapes, study prints, academic games, and a directory of producers and distributors. Coverage is increased in each successive number by adding new types of material.

COMPILATIONS

These consist of lists of selected cross-media materials on one or more subjects, with descriptive or evaluative/descriptive annotations. These exist on a variety of different subjects. Only a sampling of those which are highly selective are cited here. Many excellent lists are also compiled by state library and education associations, and by local library and school personnel.

The Elementary School Library Collection, edited by Mary V. Gaver. 4th ed. Bro-Dart Foundation, 113 Frelinghuysen Avenue, Newark, N.J. 07114. 1968. $20. Supplement. 625 pp.

> Cross-media selections are entered under Dewey classification number and integrated with books, with first, second and third purchase preference indicated. Audiovisuals are also listed separately. Each new edition reevaluates titles previously recommended and adds new ones.

Foreign Language Audio-Visual Guide, compiled and edited by Bertha Landers. Landers Associates, P.O. Box 69760, Los Angeles, Calif. 90069. 1961. 172 pp. $2.50.

> Selected instructional films, filmstrips, phonorecords, and phonotapes in twelve foreign languages, with brief content description. Additional audiovisual materials listed include flags, games, globes, maps, and charts.

A Guide to Films, Filmstrips, Maps and Globes, Records on Asia. 3d ed. The Asia Society, 112 E. 64 St., New York, N.Y. 10021. 1964. 87 pp. 50¢; minimum order, $2. Supplement, 1967.

Divided into four parts by type of medium, the titles in each part were chosen by a specialist in that type of medium. Transparencies and still pictures are included in the section on maps and globes. Brief descriptive annotations.

Instructional Materials for Teaching the Use of the Library, by Shirley L. Hopkinson. Claremont House, 231 E. San Fernando St., San Jose, Calif. 95112. 1966. 59 pp. $1.

For use at elementary, high school, and college level, this is an annotated, selected list of aids produced before September, 1965. Included among other media are films, filmstrips, phonotapes, charts, and transparencies.

⭐ *Space Science Educational Media Resources: A Guide for Junior High School Teachers,* edited by Kenneth M. McIntyre, based on a report to the National Aeronautics and Space Administration. Rev. ed. Bureau of Audiovisual Education, University of North Carolina, Chapel Hill, N.C. 27514. 1966. 89 pp. $3.50.

Correlated with the textbook *Modern Earth Science* (1961), this teaching resource guide is a cross-media compilation with descriptive/evaluative annotations of varying length. Treated here are 16mm motion pictures and filmclips, filmstrips, flat pictures, transparencies, slides, phonotapes, charts, graphs, demonstration devices, field trips, self-instruction 8mm film loops, and programmed materials. Recently produced motion pictures and filmstrips appear in a supplementary list.

Wilson

FREE MATERIALS

Free Learning Materials for Classroom Use, by Guy Wagner & Dorlan Mork. Extension Service, State College of Iowa, Cedar Falls, Iowa 50613. 1967. 81 pp. $1.50.

A list of sources, selectively chosen, for obtaining free materials. Includes a 15-point guide for the critical evaluation of materials and outlines a procedure for procuring them. Represented are industry, societies, foundations, embassies, state and other governments, and publishers. Given for each source is a complete address, brief annotation, and suggested grade levels for which its offerings are suitable.

Additional sources of critical annotations concerned with one type of material only are included in Part 2.

AID THROUGH PRODUCERS

Many producers of audiovisual materials have adopted a policy of working closely with librarians and teachers in an effort to determine what types of materials would best communicate with a variety of people, and how their products should be designed to best suit individual differences. In line with this, arrangements may be made with some producers to borrow a large selected collection (e.g., films and filmstrips), on the condition that an evaluation be made by each person using any of the material. These evaluations, returned with the collection to the producer, furnish guidance in the revision of existing products and in the creation of new ones. Advised by school and library consultants, individual producers are now furnishing graded and curriculum-oriented catalogs with good indexes and cross-references, both of which facilitate selection. Invaluable assistance is often gained, too, from producers' suggestions of how materials can be used, both separately and as correlated resources in an integrated media approach. To ensure regular receipt of current catalogs and special announcements, librarians should see that they are placed on the mailing lists of producers who supply services such as these. Should previewing be desired, the majority of producers indicate what their arrangements are in their catalogs. In some cases, detailed information and illustrations may be requested which could eliminate the necessity for previewing the actual material (e.g., Quickstrips from Eye Gate House). As in book publishing, there are certain firms that have an established reputation for quality in their production of materials in a specific medium (e.g., Dennoyer-Geppert, Nystrom, for maps and globes) or in a specialized subject area. Selection of some basic resources may be made directly from the catalogs of these companies on the strength of their past performance. Where items on a very specialized subject are required there may often be only one source for acquisition.

Producers' catalogs often list multi-media kits and/or packaged combinations of materials. These should be carefully checked both as to content and comparative costs before a purchase decision is made. Multi-media kits may often bring together some excellent resources with an equal amount of average or relatively useless material. Due consideration should be given to the quality, utility, and cost of each separate item to determine whether more benefits would be gained by selecting and purchasing them singly. Exact and accurate information on the contents of "packaged deals," often presented as correlated materials, should be researched. Close examination frequently discloses that the various items, though they may treat the same subject, either do not complement each other, or are already in the library collection, cataloged under their original publication titles.

SELECTION PROCEDURE

Since nonbook materials are an integral part of the total collection, the procedures for their selection naturally conform to the structure of already established routines. Though the detail of procedural organization may vary from library to library, the usual broad pattern of progression is based on several definite steps. These are presented here in brief form, with fuller comment devoted to those variations peculiar to nonbook materials:

- Requests for materials come from various sources, to satisfy a general or specific need.
- Determination of the need is ascertained by several methods: checking the library's resources; consulting with the originator of the request, and with specialists; estimating the durability and priority of the need.
- Information on materials available is researched.

Utilizing selection aids, materials are evaluated on the basis of accepted selection criteria. To avoid repetition of effort completed evaluations should be kept on file and checked when materials are requested. Existing evaluation forms for books may be revised for nonbook materials, or new ones designed.

As a guide in evaluation form composition the sample shows the salient points that should be included, all of them related to the criteria previously discussed. It is intended for the coverage of all nonbook ma-

---

NONBOOK MATERIALS EVALUATION FORM

TITLE _____

Circle TYPE OF MATERIAL: Chart: Film: 16mm.,
8mm.; Filmstrip; Globe; Kit; Map;
Picture; Programmed material;
Record: disc, tape; Slide; Transparency;

PRODUCER/DISTRIBUTOR   DATE

Other_____

COST   TECHNICAL DESCRIPTION _____

CONTENT SUMMARY:

Check where applicable:
AUTHENTICITY: accurate; impartial; up-
   to-date.
APPROPRIATENESS: in vocabulary concepts;
   data; relation of media to subject.
SCOPE: content; concepts; communication.
INTEREST: credibility; stimulation;
   imagination, human, sensory appeal.
ORGANIZATION: logical; balanced.
TECHNICAL ASPECTS: tone; clarity; focus;
   composition; color; synchronization.
SPECIAL FEATURES: notes; guides; accom-
   panying material.
PHYSICAL CHARACTERISTICS: for ease of
   use; storage; durability.

Excellent	Good	Poor

Circle possible LIBRARY USES: Individual; Group; Disadvantaged; Introduction; Study in
                depth; Overview; Other_____

COMMENTS:

RECOMMENDED FOR PURCHASE: _____   _____   _____
                              Yes   No   Defer

EVALUATOR   POSITION   DATE

Insert additional items for school libraries:
Circle GRADE RANGE: K 1 2 3 4 5 6 7 8 9 10 11 12; Parent Ed.; Teacher.

Circle CURRICULUM AREAS: Lang. Arts; Social Studies; Math; Science; Art; Music; P.E.
                Other_____

FORM 1. NONBOOK MATERIALS EVALUATION FORM

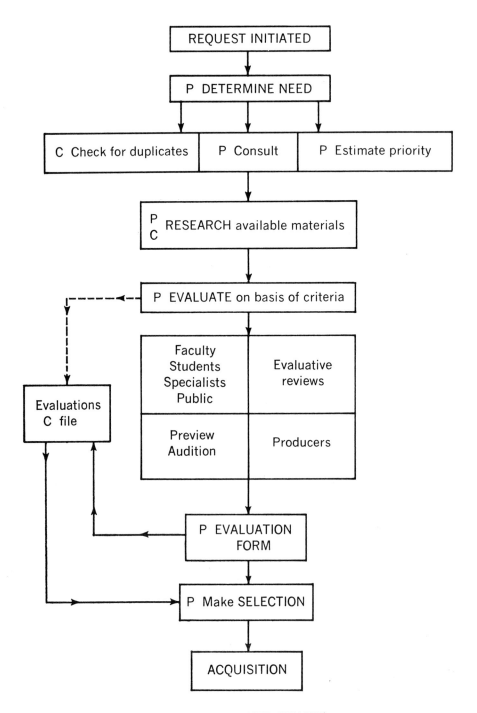

CODE: C—Clerical procedures
P—Professional procedures
————Alternate procedures

REQUEST INITIATED

P DETERMINE NEED

C Check for duplicates | P Consult | P Estimate priority

P
C RESEARCH available materials

P EVALUATE on basis of criteria

Faculty
Students
Specialists
Public

Evaluative
reviews

Preview
Audition

Producers

Evaluations
C file

P EVALUATION
FORM

P Make SELECTION

ACQUISITION

FIGURE 12. SELECTION WORK-FLOW CHART

terials and does not itemize information pertaining to specific types of materials. Such detail should be incorporated if a separate evaluation form is desired for each of the various kinds of resources.

After evaluation, selection is made. To qualify a product for purchase, a set number of evaluations may be needed, and one or more persons or committees may be made responsible for the final decision.

Acquisition procedure is started.

BIBLIOGRAPHY

Allison, Mary L., comp. *New Educational Materials.* New York: Citation Press, 1968.

"EPIE: Educational Products Information Exchange." *Audiovisual Instruction* 12, No. 4 (April 1967): 382–383.

Geller, Evelyn. "Small Ways Out of Chaos." *School Library Journal* 14 (Nov. 1967): 19.

Lane, David O. "The Selection of Academic Library Materials; A Literature Survey." *College & Research Libraries* 29, No. 5 (Sept. 1968): 364–372.

"Nonprint Media: A New Reviewing Service." *The Booklist* 66 (Sept. 1, 1969): 34–35.

Quinly, William J. "The Selection, Processing and Storage of Non-Print Materials: Aids, Indexes and Guidelines." *Library Trends* 16, No. 2 (Oct. 1967): 274–282.

Rufsvold, Margaret I., and Carolyn Guss. *Guides to Newer Educational Media: Films, Filmstrips, Kinescopes, Phonodiscs, Phonotapes, Programmed Instruction Materials, Slides, Transparencies, Videotapes.* 2nd ed. Chicago: A.L.A., 1967.

4

WAYS AND MEANS
OF ACQUISITION

GUIDELINES AND POLICIES

Every library has acquisition procedures, and the librarian, already familiar with these, need only adapt them to the acquisition of nonbook materials. Preplanning this incorporation into the existing system minimizes confusion and ensures efficiency of operation, and it must be kept in mind that flexibility in routines is required to handle audiovisual products. The new acquisition procedures must accommodate themselves to the unique features of audiovisual materials, and these should be identified as far as possible in adapting already accepted ordering procedures.

Structurally, acquisition is considered a separate process concerned with the ordering and receiving of materials through purchase, rental, free loan, gift, or local production: it begins when selection is completed. However, it does play an important role in carrying out the function of the modern library, and, in many respects, is intertwined with selection. Determination of some basic acquisition policies clearly hinges upon selection objectives, criteria, and decisions.

The high cost of some nonbook materials, even though evaluated as excellent, imposes limitations on their purchase. One 16mm color motion picture, for example, may cost $500, which could represent a disproportionate expenditure of funds. In such instances the desired material may have to be obtained through rental. Judgments concerning the advisability of rental or purchase should be based on an accepted formulated policy that reflects some of the factors that influence selection. If a 16mm film is called for only once or twice a year, rental is the best approach. On the other hand, purchase is recommended if the film is requested ten times a year, or the importance of having it in the collection to meet immediate needs has been demonstrated.

A considerable volume of nonbook material may be procured for demonstration on a free loan, short- or long-term basis. A definite policy should be stated covering the acquisition of sponsored, free loan, and gift materials. It should be clearly understood that such items must contribute to furthering the objectives of the library and be subject to the same evaluative criteria and selection procedures as are those which are reviewed for permanent addition to the collection. Nor should they constitute an excuse for limiting the budget, as sufficient funds should be provided to obviate the necessity of relying on these materials as substitutes for superior ones available through regular purchase.

Interrelationships between acquisition and selection are evident in accomplishing and maintaining balance in the collection. Since this concerns both type of material and subject area, it demands flexibility in acquisition policies. To meet the diversity of patron needs the basic collection of nonbook materials should include a wide variety of media which may range from the usual recordings to the unusual three-dimensional resources. Which type of material and the rate at which each should be acquired rest upon the selector's knowledge of the people whom the library reaches out to serve. The budget, however, delineates realistic boundaries to the size of the collection of any particular type of nonbook material. In addition, changes in technology also affect the extent of purchase of specific kinds of resources. The development of equipment which permits easy and frequent use of a material by the indivdiual is a valid indicator that an increased amount of that material should be acquired. The enlargement of the filmstrip collection, for example, is warranted by the availability of very inexpensive projectors which can be checked out to the patron for home use. Subject balance also depends upon the selector, upon his familiarity with available materials, and his continuous evaluation of the entire collection in relation to the objectives of the library and its patrons' needs. For guidance on the size of nonbook collections both the new *Standards for School Media Programs* developed jointly by the A.L.A. American Association of School Librarians and the N.E.A. Department of Audiovisual Instruction and state and local standards should be consulted.

BUDGET PLANNING AND PREPARATION

To best fill clientele demands within the confines of the budget, funds should be allocated for the purchase, rental and production of materials. A further breakdown for book and nonbook expenditures is made in the purchasing category. Here, again, basic relationships to the overall function of the library are evident, as such a division creates a balance which directly reflects the needs of the library's patrons. As a rule, the larger portion of the budget should be devoted to purchase. The amount ear-marked for rental need be sufficient only to procure items whose cost is excessive, or which need expensive equipment and extraordinary maintenance. To take care of specific requirements which cannot be met by commercial products, funds should be set aside to buy raw materials such as blank audio and video tapes, film for slides, and supplies for transparencies. These resources may be made by the library or by the patron, and become part of the permanent nonbook collection.

A proven and practical procedure for budget preparation is the "work plan." Through this method, structured on the basic steps of policy determination, research, and work estimate, the final budget statement evolves.

The planning of any program must be guided by approved policies. Since the majority of these are usually well established, library personnel should already understand them, or have little difficulty in becoming familiar with them. Fiscal and administrative policies, and even local, state, and national laws, all constitute the framework on which any project is built. Other policies which were not previously needed may have to be formulated before actual planning begins. These often pertain to specific library procedures which can affect the program. An audiovisual resources circulation policy, for instance, should be determined from the very beginning. The decision on whether or not some easily damaged materials, such as phonograph records, should be circulated outside the library will certainly have a direct bearing on budget estimate. As planning progresses, additional policies may have to be set to handle those facets which are not initially apparent but continue to emerge as important considerations.

Research involves both evaluation of the collection and understanding of the present and possible future needs of the patron. This knowledge should be readily available through the selection process. Up-to-date information on audiovisual materials and equipment is also needed to make those valid comparisons on which purchase recommendations are based. Under consideration, too, should be changes in materials and equipment which could result in improvement or extension of services, with consequent budget revision.

To be feasible, budget estimates must be based not only on policy and research, but also on carefully thought-through plans clearly formulated to indicate the accomplishments intended for the future. Both short and long term achievements are spelled out, some being scheduled for one or two years, others for from five to ten years. A budget file is then set up that is a practical translation of these plans. Division of this file into sections for short- and long-term commitment makes it an efficient tool. In the first is placed every item and suggestion that, according to plan, should be considered for the next fiscal period. In the second are entered those that will be handled in more than one year. Some of the latter could require more extensive research and program development for their justification, as, for example, the installation of a television system. This file should be started at least one year in advance of the budget submittal date to allow sufficient time to gather together necessary information, review it, and select from it the essentials which will complete the work projected for the following year. The expenditures for this work are then estimated and final revisions are made if some items are so exorbitant that the total oversteps reasonable limits. Through this procedure a budget document has evolved which indicates the funds needed to carry out a definite program of work for a fiscal period.

BUSINESS MANAGEMENT

Once the budget has been adopted, budget control methods need no adaptation to cover different kinds of materials. The same forms, mode of expenditure entry, and accounting techniques that provide a running balance and up-to-date information on encumbrances in the book budget perform equally well for non-book allocations.

Although multi-media acquisition does not require different means of purchasing and accounting, handling the peculiarities of audiovisual materials in ordering and receiving does necessitate some retailoring of forms and methods. No departure from basic routines is involved. However, this adaptation presents an excellent opportunity for an objective reexamination of established procedures. By applying that fundamental principle of business management that advocates the reduction of all procedures and techniques to their simplest form, some revisions may appear advisable. Since complexity in routines can insidiously increase costs, the steps in existing ordering and receiving procedures, as well as any additional ones considered, should be evaluated by carefully weighing their real accomplishment against the expense they produce in materials and personnel time.

BUYING GUIDES

The business skills employed in book buying are practiced even more extensively in nonbook purchasing. In the book field the pattern of procurement from publishers and/or vendors is well established. As a rule, the library need deal with only a few companies since one jobber can provide the publications of most of the major firms. The librarian soon becomes familiar with the different discounts, services, and delivery guarantees offered and can keep abreast of any developments which might affect the library's acquisitions. In selecting purchase sources he applies his business skill in analyzing various factors and combining them to obtain the best supply for the most economical price.

In the nonbook realm the acquisition picture is much more confused. Audiovisuals, as relative newcomers, have not been in demand long enough to warrant the formation of easily recognizable shopping patterns. Consequently, the majority of them must be purchased directly from each producer. This lack of centralized vending multiplies the work and expense of acquisition. In addition, the tremendous production impetus in recent years has resulted from the rapid emergence of new companies and a variety of changes in previously familiar ones. In many instances this instability demands the expenditure of a considerable amount of time in research before the best ordering source can be determined.

Since an audiovisual reference tool comparable to *Books in Print* has not yet appeared, an up-to-date file of producers' catalogs must act as a substitute. The multipurpose use of producers' catalogs in selection and in cataloging, as well as in acquisition, is ample justification for keeping them. The coverage of this collection will rapidly widen by the librarian's requesting that the library be placed on producers' mailing lists, by responding to advertisements, contacting salesmen, and attending conference exhibits.

To become familiar with the various sources of supply, producers' catalogs are indispensable. They are, however, a source of frustration when one is searching for the specifics required in acquisition. Such information may be found more readily by consulting several publications which are, in essence, partial indexes to producers' catalogs. These vary in type according to their indexing approach. They may appear as separate directories, lists of recommended sources, descriptive compilations of selected or comprehensive single or multi-media; or, they may present a combination of many of these elements in one volume. Since the acquisition of all these reference tools could become disproportionately expensive, and since there is a certain amount of overlap in the knowledge they furnish, it is advisable to examine them critically and choose those which, together, will provide the maximum of information. Some of the principal ones listed here supplement those already noted in the previous chapter on selection. Additional source guides are included in the treatment of cataloging, physical processing, equipment, and specific types of materials.

SOURCE GUIDES

AVI Guide to New Products. Department of Audiovisual Instruction, National Education Association, 1201 16th St., N.W., Washington, D.C. 20036. Annual.

Since 1967 this compilation has been included in the September issue of *Audiovisual Instruction* as a detachable supplement. It is a partial listing of products released since the previous April, or to be released during the current school year. Names and addresses of producers are given as well as full descriptions of the audiovisual products, which include source books, materials, equipment, and supplies.

Audiovisual Market Place, edited by Olga S. Weber. N.Y.: R. R. Bowker, 1969.

A directory of the audiovisual industry listing people and places, organizations and services, conventions and trade events, and publications concerned with the new media, films, filmstrips, film loops, slides, tapes, transparencies, maps and globes. This directory can be up-dated by adding new entries which appear in the "Advertisers Index" of *Audiovisual Instruction* and in the "Audiovisual Directory: Producers and Distributors," included in "The Audiovisual Guide: A Multimedia Subject List" of *School Library Journal.*

Blue Book of Audiovisual Materials. Educational Screen & Audiovisual Guide, 434 S. Wabash, Chicago, Ill. 60605. Annual.

Available separately, or with the August issue of *Educational Screen and Audiovisual Guide.* Arranged alphabetically by subject, with a title index, it covers motion pictures, filmstrips, slides, disc and tape recordings, and features a directory of listed sources.

NICEM Index to 16mm Educational Films, compiled by the National Information Center for Educational Media of the University of Southern California. 2nd ed. New York: Bowker, 1969.

NICEM Index to 8mm Educational Motion Cartridges, compiled by the National Information Center for Educational Media of the University of Southern California. New York: Bowker, 1969.

NICEM Index to 35mm Educational Filmstrips, compiled by the National Information Center for Educational Media of the University of Southern California. 2nd ed. New York: Bowker, 1969.

NICEM Index to Overhead Transparencies, compiled by the National Information Center for Educational Media of the University of Southern California. New York: Bowker, 1969.

These volumes present the titles stored in the NICEM computer bank and provide the most complete availability information on the four types of media. Each book is divided into three main sections: a subject guide, with overview categories, specific topics, and alphabetical subject areas; an alphabetical guide by title, with full bibliographical data, physical description, and Library of Congress card number (where available); a directory of producers and distributors, with complete addresses, indexed both by name and code.

The PRIME Catalog. Totowa, N.J.: Educators PRIME Information Service (a division of Hutton Publishing Co.), 1969.

It is intended that this catalog be placed in central county schools throughout the country to provide an instructional materials reference center for each 150 teachers in any school system. It is a compilation of more than 15,000 listings of products and services, identified by subject area, instructional level and methodology, with an index by products and one that will lead to products and services from a delineation of pupil characteristics.

FREE MATERIALS SOURCE GUIDES

Educators Progress Service, Randolph, Wis. 53956. This company publishes annually several guides to materials which are free or available for loan free of charge. They cover both single and multimedia on a variety of subjects. Each one is indexed by source and availability, title and subject. Some of the titles are: *Educators' Guide to Free Films; Educators' Guide to Free Filmstrips; Educators' Guide to Free Guidance Materials; Educators' Guide to Free Science Materials; Educators' Guide to Free Social Studies Materials; Educators' Guide to Free Tapes, Scripts, and Transcriptions; Elementary Teachers' Guide to Free Curriculum Materials.*

Free and Inexpensive Learning Materials. Division of Surveys and Field Services, George Peabody College for Teachers, Nashville, Tenn., 37203.

Revised biennially in the even numbered years.

Sangamon Source Series, Villa Grove, Ill. Any of the following titles may be procured for $.99 each or five for $4:

Free Guidance Materials—Trades; Free Guidance Materials—Professions; Free Materials About Foreign Countries; Free Materials About Our National Parks, Forests, and Historic Sites; Free Materials of Our Fifty States; Free Posters, Charts, and Maps; Free Sources of Science Materials.

What's Free. Sangamon Source Series, Villa Grove, Ill. Quarterly. $3. Describes all kinds of free materials currently available for schools and libraries.

Sources of Free and Inexpensive Educational Materials. Esther Dever, P.O. Box 186 Grafton, W.Va.

Sources of Free and Inexpensive Teaching Aids. Bruce Miller Publications, P.O. Box 369, Riverside, Calif. 92502.

Sources of Information and Unusual Services. Informational Directory Co., 200 West 57th St., New York, N.Y. 10019.

To dispel some of the confusion in the selection and acquisition of audiovisual products there seems to be a concerted cooperative effort to establish coordination between producers and customers. This trend is noticeable in the formation of large centers such as the American Education Center planned for downtown Atlanta. This will be maintained on a twelve-month basis, and will house all types of educational materials, equipment, services and supplies, as well as provide rooms for demonstrations, sales presentations, workshops, seminars, symposiums and roundtable discussions. The National Audiovisual Center (serviced through the National Archives and Records Service, General Services Administration), has been established in Washington, D.C., to coordinate information, sales, and distribution for all government audiovisual materials. Information on all pictures, filmstrips, slide sets, audio and video tapes, and special audiovisual packets produced by or for the federal agencies, is made available on request to educational institutions, commercial companies and individuals. A sales catalog describing over 5,000 U.S. Government audiovisual materials may be purchased from the Center.

The use of carefully selected source guides facilitates acquisition research. Indispensable for efficient preparation of requisitions, however, is a quick reference tool that will supply at a glance all the ordering details required. A producer/vendor card file makes this "fingertip knowledge" readily accessible. Such a file is easy to handle, occupies a minimum of space, and may be placed on or close to the typing desk.

This file should be planned for and initiated with the first order placed for nonbook materials. It consists of a compilation of cards, alphabetically arranged by producer. Each one represents a company from which the library has, or will procure materials, and summarizes all the information considered essential for ordering. Entries may be made on standard 3x5 cards, or on those that fit a Rolodex file, if one is available.

Once the file has been started it should be updated by scanning producers' catalogs as they are received, and adding entries or revising existing ones as needed. Appropriate cross-references should be made for divisions of parent companies, name changes, local representatives, distributors, and dealers. Experience has shown that the time required for card preparation for this file is far less than that spent in searching out comparable information every time an order is placed. It generates additional economy since it indicates single sources for obtaining materials produced by several companies, thus minimizing the number of transactions needed.

The information recorded on the card should include:

Producers' name and address, with zip code. Include name abbreviations or codes, which should conform to those used in cataloging.

Producer's catalog on file. This may be indicated by noting the catalog year date in pencil in the upper right corner of the card. Revision of this date upon the receipt of a new catalog provides an up-to-date index to the producers' catalog collection.

Types of material which the firm supplies. These may be listed on the right hand quarter of the card where there is sufficient space for additions and deletions.

Local representative's name and address.

Distributors. The company may be a distributor for the products of other firms, or its own materials may be distributed by another producer. Cross-references should be made here.

Dealers or vendors. The majority of jobbers specialize in one type of material, such as phonograph records. Currently, however, there is an increase in the number of vendors who, like those who handle books, will furnish the products of several different companies. These should be cross-referenced since the fewer the number of orders processed the greater the economy of operation.

Business arrangements:

Prices: net; discounts. Net prices are usually quoted for nonbook materials. Discounts are available for some, such as records and art prints, and for large quantity purchases.

Policies of the company regarding: return and replacement of imperfect items or those damaged in shipment; replacement of materials damaged through use; exchange privileges subsequent to evaluation; on-approval or preview availability.

Service pertaining to: delivery time guarantee; promptness in rectifying errors; provision of teacher's guides to materials as advertised, and in sufficient quantity; servicing contracts for equipment; invoicing peculiarities.

Cataloging: availability of catalog card and physical processing kits; provision of L.C. card numbers for materials cataloged by the Library of Congress.

All this information, of course, may not be applicable or required for every producer. Each library must evaluate and determine the information needed in its own acquisition processing, and record only those items which will be of benefit. The following examples illustrate possible entries for one producer.

---

[1]SOCIETY FOR VISUAL EDUCATION, INC.   [9]SVE   [10] '70
[2]1345 Diversey Parkway
  Chicago, Illinois 60614   8 mm.
[3]Subsidiary of General Precision   equipment
    Equipment Corp.   filmstrips
                                                    kits
[4]Kenneth E. Clouse   records   11
  223 Quail Hollow Road   slides
  Felton, California 95018   storage-
                                                      units
[5]Net   study-
[6]15-day approval   prints
[7]No replacement   supplies
[8]Cataloging kits

---

[1] Name	[5] Price	[9] Abbreviation
[2] Address	[6] Preview	[10] Catalog
[3] Parent Co.	[7] Policy	[11] Type of
[4] Local representative	[8] Cataloging & processing	Material

FORM 2. PRODUCER'S CARD FOR ACQUISITION QUICK-REFERENCE FILE

```
CLOUSE, KENNETH E.
223 Quail Hollow Road
Felton, California  95018

Rep:  SVE
Dist:  IMED
```

FORM 3. LOCAL REPRESENTATIVE'S CARD FOR ACQUISITION
    QUICK-REFERENCE FILE

```
General Precision and Equipment Corp.

    see

SOCIETY FOR VISUAL EDUCATION, INC.
```

FORM 4. CROSS-REFERENCE CARD FOR ACQUISITION QUICK-
    REFERENCE FILE

```
INSTRUCTIONAL MATERIALS AND EQUIPMENT     IMED      \70
   DISTRIBUTORS.
P.O. Box 49967                                     study-
Los Angeles, Calif.  90049                         prints


Dist:   Kenneth E. Clouse
        223 Quail Hollow Road
        Felton, California  95018
```

FORM 5. PRODUCER'S CARD FOR ACQUISITION QUICK-REFERENCE
       FILE, SHOWING A DISTRIBUTOR COMMON TO ANOTHER
       COMPANY

ORDERING AND RECEIVING

The ordering and receiving routines here recommended for nonbook materials are based on the use of a multiple-copy order form. The 5-part order form used in this book was designed to accommodate the new Library of Congerss card order form. The composition of the first slip meets the Library's specifications for optical scanning and is used for ordering Library of Congress cards. The items on the remaining four slips, used to order the materials, have been arranged so that only one typing is needed to enter information for ordering both L.C. cards and the material itself.

The procedure is simple, yet comprehensive enough to be suitable for a single library of any size, a district processing center, or a regional system facility. Since the various steps are identical to those followed in a book acquisition, a detailed description of each is not needed. Highlighted are only those variations which pertain specifically to audiovisual resources. Where certain techniques are explained more fully, the intent is to reemphasize the interrelationships among various library processes, such as selection, acquisition and cataloging, which should function in every well administered library.

✓   The request for acquisition proceeds directly from selection. For efficiency and economy in a multi-library system it should be prepared on the 5-part order form, with the maximum of information recorded. Where selection has been made from preview such details as catalog number, producer, etc., can be easily noted from the material in

SUBSCRIBER NO.	Hold C	L.C. PREFIX	L.C. CARD NUMBER
167205	3	Fil	—

FOR	AUTHOR (LAST NAME FIRST)	
DEALER	TITLE Japan: Hiroshima and Osaka	1
	284-7	2
NO. OF COPIES		3
		4
LIST PRICE	PUBLISHER PUB. DATE EDITION OR BINDING	5
	Chicago: SVE 1968	6
DATE ORDERED	RECOMMENDED:	
	NOW LIB/-H/4SA	

Ⓟ • □ □ □ □ □ □ □ □ □ □—□ □ □ □ □

A B C D E F G SBN **H I J K L M N O**

FORM 6. OPTICAL LIBRARY OF CONGRESS CARD-ORDER FORM
DESIGNED AS THE FIRST SLIP OF A MULTIPLE-COPY
BOOK ORDER FORM. Cards ordered by title without L.C. card
number. Cards for a filmstrip. (*Form courtesy of Moore Business
Forms, Inc.*)

REQUESTED BY:	COST PRICE	ACTION
A.M. Tillin		

FOR	COMPOSER, ARTIST		
Soc. St.			
	TITLE; NO. & TYPE OF MATERIAL		
	Japan: Hiroshima and Osaka: 1 filmstrip,		
NO. OF COPIES	1 record, 1 guide		
1			
LIST PRICE	PRODUCER	DATE	CATALOG NO.
9.50	SVE	1968	284-7; 284-4RR
DATE ORDERED	RECOMMENDED:		
1/15/69	Preview		

LIBRARY
Address

AV PURCHASE REQUEST

FORM 7. AUDIOVISUAL PURCHASE REQUEST FORM
(*Form courtesy of Moore Business Forms, Inc.*)

hand. The requestor keeps the fourth slip and forwards the remaining four slips to acquisition.

If the multiple-copy form is not used, as in a single library, a purchase request card should be provided. Those particulars that relate only to acquisition, such as dealer and date received, need not appear on it. However, if the items retained are placed on the card in the same position and sequence as are those on the multiple-copy order form, subsequent typing for completion of the order will be facilitated.

Complete the order information on the form. Check for duplication. If it has not already been done in selection, the public catalog and permanent order file should be checked to avoid duplication.

Compile the bibliographic data. The producer's catalog is the most complete source for providing bibliographic data, catalog numbers, composition of sets, prices, and title verification. A glance at the upper right corner of the producer's card in the quick reference file will indicate if a catalog is on file. Since similarities in titles often occur in audiovisual materials, identification by catalog number will minimize confusion and errors. By specifying, after the title, the types of material and how many are supposed to be included, both the checking upon receipt and the subsequent cataloging will be much easier and speedier. If a particular format is desired it should be clearly stated. Standard 8mm films, for example, will be sent unless Super 8 is requested.

Determine the vendor and secure purchase order number.

Library of Congress card numbers. If Library of Congress cards are not ordered, the first slip of the multiple order form should be removed before typing begins. It should be retained for possible future use. If L.C. cards, available for films, filmstrips and records, are to be ordered, the first slip remains in its place. The L.C. card numbers, secured from the National Union Catalogs or from lists supplied by certain producers (see Ordering L.C. Cards, Chapter 6) should be inserted.

The library book order form is accepted by all producers and may be used without revision for ordering nonbook materials. The information is placed on it as shown in the sample. Or, if desired, a special form in the same layout may be designed for audiovisual orders.

Prepare the requisition. There is no need to list titles on the requisition. The statement that items be supplied "as per attached slips" suffices. Where applicable, discounts, delivery dates, exchange arrangements, and special shipping or invoicing instructions should be noted.

The second slip of each 5-part form used is removed. These are alphabetized or otherwise arranged as required by the vendor, and are attached to the requisition, which is then sent to the purchasing section. Slip 3 is filed by purchase order number to await receipt of the order. Slip 4, in a multi-library system, is retained by the requestor. If a purchase request card is used, Slip 4 is filed with Slip 3. Slip 5 is filed in the Permanent Order file.

When the material is received, it is checked against the slips in the Purchase Order Number File and against the invoice, and the date of receipt is noted. It is then checked for damage. Extensive checking for damage of audiovisual products is neither logistically nor economically feasible. Since monitoring these materials involves special equipment and an excessive amount of time, only a cursory inspection can be made. If damage becomes evident during processing or patron use, adjustment

P.O. NUMBER	CLASS NO.	COST PRICE	CANCELLED		DATE REC'D.
61248			OP. OS.		

FOR	AUTHOR LAST NAME FIRST		
Soc. St.			
DEALER	**TITLE**		
SVE	Japan: Hiroshima and Osaka: 1 filmstrip,		
NO. OF COPIES	1 record, 1 guide		
1			
LIST PRICE	PUBLISHER	PUB. DATE	EDITION OR BINDING
9.50	SVE	1968	284-7; 284-4RR
DATE ORDERED	RECOMMENDED:		
1/16/69	Preview A.M.T.		

LIBRARY
Address   **LIBRARY BOOK ORDER**

FORM 8. AUDIOVISUAL MATERIALS ORDERED ON BOOK
ORDER FORM (*Form courtesy of Moore Business Forms, Inc.*)

P.O. NUMBER	CLASS NO.	COST PRICE	CANCELLED		DATE REC'D.
61248			OP. OS.		

FOR	COMPOSER, ARTIST		
Soc. St.			
DEALER	**TITLE; NO. & TYPE OF MATERIAL**		
SVE	Japan: Hiroshima and Osaka: 1 filmstrip,		
NO. OF COPIES	1 record, 1 guide		
1			
LIST PRICE	PRODUCER	DATE	CATALOG NO.
9.50	SVE	1968	284-7; 284-4RR
DATE ORDERED	RECOMMENDED:		
1/16/69	Preview A.M.T.		

LIBRARY
Address   **LIBRARY AV ORDER**

FORM 9. AUDIOVISUALS ORDER FORM (*Form courtesy of
Moore Business Forms, Inc.*)

LIBRARY
Address

Date _____

Vendor:

Gentlemen:

Please expedite as indicated below:

ACCOUNT NUMBER	P. O. NUMBER	YOUR INVOICE NUMBER	DATE OF INVOICE
COPIES	AUTHOR AND TITLE	PRICE	DISCOUNT	CREDIT

Coordinator Library Services

Action Requested Please:	Material Returned Reason:	Adjustment Needed Reason:
.... Send item(s)	.... Imperfect/damaged	.... Price incorrect
.... Send on approval	.... Binding/container not acceptable	.... Extension incorrect
.... Send review copy	.... Incorrect title	.... Send corrected invoice
.... Send information	.... Incorrect author	.... Billed but not received
.... Replace	.... Too many copies	.... Send credit memo
.... Cancel	.... Not ordered	.... Received but not billed
.... Other:	.... Received after order closed	.... Send billing
	.... Review/approval copy	.... Billed but not correct title
	.... Other:	.... Other:

FORM 10. REQUISITION OR REPORT TO VENDOR FORM
(Form courtesy of Moore Business Forms, Inc.)

from the vendor can be sought at this later date. As a rule, if it is evident that the material is new, the majority of producers will replace damaged or imperfect materials even though they have been processed by the library.

Errors in shipments and/or billing should be reported to the vendor

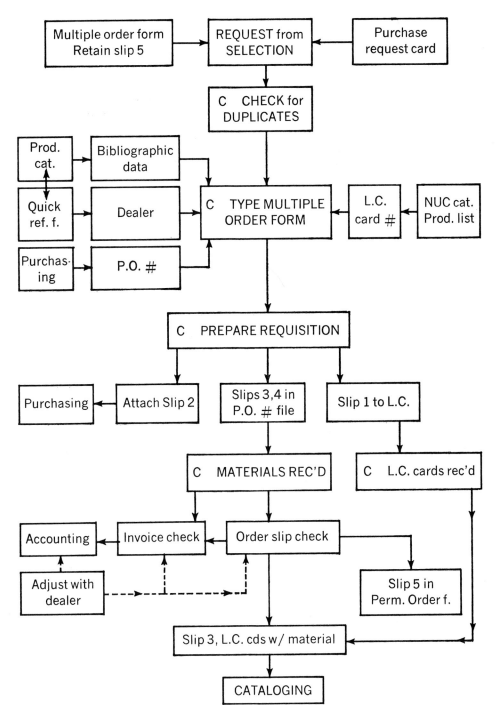

CODE: C—Clerical procedures
P—Professional procedures
— — — —Alternate procedures

FIGURE 13. ACQUISITION WORK FLOW CHART

as rapidly as possible. A standardized, preprinted form requiring a minimum of typing should be designed for this purpose. The one shown in this section may be used for both books and audiovisual materials, either as a requisition or a report to the vendor.

Slip 3 should accompany the material to the cataloging and processing section as a cataloging workslip. If Slip 4 was filed with Slip 3, it may be returned to the originator of the request as a notice that the material is ready for use. If Library of Congress Cards have been received, they should also be pulled and routed with the material.

Invoices and purchase orders are signed, routed, and filed according to established practices.

BIBLIOGRAPHY

American Library Association and the National Education Association. *Standards for School Media Programs*. Prepared by a Joint Committee of the American Association of School Librarians and the Department of Audiovisual Instruction. Chicago: A.L.A., 1969.

Carr, Patrick. "Using Free Printed Materials Effectively." *Audiovisual Instruction* 13, No. 1 (Jan. 1968): 60–63.

Geller, Evelyn. "Crisis in Red and Black." *School Library Journal* 16 (Sept. 1969): 40–44.

"It's Happening." *Educational Product Report* 2, No. 1 (Oct. 1968): 6–7.

Rowell, John. "AASL and DAVI Issue New Standards for Media Programs." *The Instructor* 78, No. 3 (Nov. 1969): 81–85.

Schramm, Wilbur. *The New Media: Memo to Educational Planners*. Paris: International Institute for Educational Planning, 1968.

Wittich, Walter Arno, and Charles Francis Schuller. *Audiovisual Materials: Their Nature and Use*. 4th ed. New York: Harper & Row, 1967.

The Appendix of this book is a well selected source list for all types of materials, equipment, and supplies.

5

DECISIONS FOR
MATERIALS ORGANIZATION

The aim of each service agency in providing multi-media materials is to facilitate communication of ideas to the individual. This objective, even though it may not be implemented to its fullest extent immediately, is fundamental in formulating rules for procedural routines. Nor can these rules be so rigid that they become an end in themselves. They must be flexible enough to adapt to ever-changing conditions of growth, physical facilities, materials integration, and use. The organization must be equal to these changes or efforts are wasted.

Specifically, organization encompasses all those processes employed in preparing materials for patron use. With the acquisition of resources it is imperative to think through the complete organization from cataloging through circulation, visualizing how the various procedures should coordinate smoothly. Before beginning the actual cataloging and processing of nonbook materials certain policy decisions which will directly affect their treatment must be made. If these are not clearly determined and understood initially, confusion is apt to result. The topics discussed in the following paragraphs are those that relate particularly to the choice of cataloging and processing methods.

CIRCULATION POLICIES

Several interrelated factors peculiar to nonbook materials will influence circulation policy decisions.

First, the format may dictate circulation rules specific to the type of material. Those items that are easily portable and present no packaging problems (e.g., tapes, filmstrips) may be circulated to individuals for use outside the library. Those that, because of fragility, size, weight or shape, require extraordinary containers or special handling (e.g., models, mock-ups, art objects), may be provided for use only within the library.

Second, the projected use or purpose of each type of media may affect the length of loan period. The viewing of a filmstrip might require only a two-hour or overnight check-out time. The studying of an art print might necessitate a two-week (or longer) loan period. The number of items of each type of material provided as compared to frequency of use influences the length of circulation time. As the collection grows materials may be loaned for a more extended period. As with printed materials, temporary or permanent restrictions may be placed on the availability of certain items by limiting them to reference, reserve, or faculty use only.

Next, the initial cost and subsequent expense for damage repair of certain types of relatively fragile material may govern circulation policies. Damage may easily result from rough handling, improper equipment and ignorance in the use of reproducing machines. Wide circulation of such materials necessitates inspection and repair upon return, which requires personnel time and special equipment. If these are not available the expense of providing frequent replacement of damaged items will have to be accepted as one of the overhead costs of the program.

Fourth, the economic level of the community that the library serves has a direct bearing on the circulation of audiovisual materials. The incidence of suitable audiovisual equipment in the home will vary according to the wealth of the neighborhood. If the library cannot provide a projector or tape recorder for home use, the borrower who does not have this equipment in his home can gain little from the collection of filmstrips or tapes.

Finally, in weighing these various factors, it is recommended that serious consideration be given to the learning experiences implicit in patron handling and access to materials. The educational value of these materials to individuals using them outside the library should not be negated because of the difficulties involved in processing and controlling them.

EQUIPMENT FOR THE INDIVIDUAL

Individual viewing and listening require special facilities, equipment, and instruction different from those provided for group use. Mechanisms for room darkening and separate sound systems, essential for independent use of audiovisual materials, are often difficult to obtain in a traditional library. It is important that equipment intended for individual use either in the library or in the home be simple to operate. Consideration should be given to the amount of operating instruction necessary for each person who wishes to check out audiovisual equipment. Fortunately machines are currently being produced that are admirably suited to individual use since they emphasize such features as automatic threading, earphones, compactness and light weight.

Inherent in the increased circulation of audiovisual materials is the provision of equipment for use outside the library. The amount and kind of equipment circulated may often be determined by the home facilities available for reproduction. While many people may have their own record players, fewer would be able to furnish a projector for film, filmstrip, or slide viewing.

Decisions as to the type of equipment allowed to circulate will be controlled to a great extent by the initial cost of equipment and the increased expense for maintenance, repair, and supplies, such as projection lamps and reels. While the

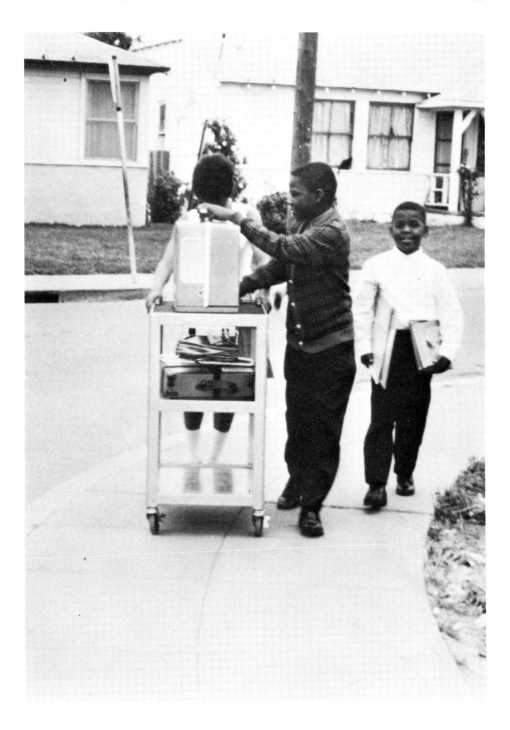

FIGURE 14. CIRCULATION OF 16MM PROJECTORS. *Where there's a will, there's a way. Costly and cumbersome 16mm projectors can be checked out for circulation.* (Photograph courtesy of the Oakland, California, Public Schools.)

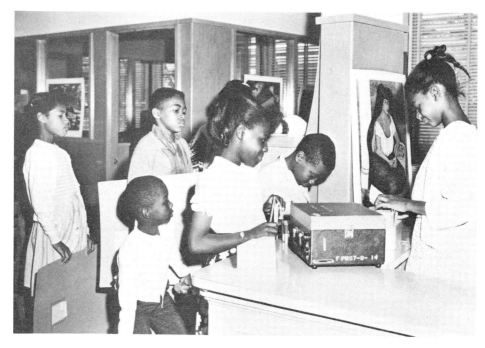

FIGURE 15. CIRCULATION OF AUDIOVISUAL EQUIPMENT. *New atti-tudes toward circulation permit library patrons to use nonbook materials at home.* (Photograph courtesy of Oakland, California, Public Schools.)

budget may be able to provide some lightweight inexpensive filmstrip projectors for circulation it may not be able to support the lending of costly and cumbersome 16mm projectors.

COLLECTION INTEGRATION

STORAGE FACILITIES

The storage of audiovisual materials of many different shapes and sizes may have to be regulated by the available physical facilities. Ideally, nonbook and print materials should be shelved together. Such an integrated collection permits the searcher to see rapidly all the different types of materials available to meet his immediate need. This wide choice generates new ideas and minimizes the frustration resulting from the necessity for further search and delay. Ingenuity on the part of the librarian and the progress presently being made toward modular packaging of audiovisual materials may accomplish the desired integration. Items such as filmstrips, films, tapes, kits and records may feasibly be shelved with books. Other materials such as art prints, specimens, charts and models may have to be placed contiguously in specialized shelving. Such an integrated collection, permitting free patron access, requires the use of the same classification system for book and nonbook materials. Local conditions and physical facilities may demand

FIGURE 16. AUDIOVISUAL EQUIPMENT AND INDEPENDENT VIEW-ING. *Individual viewing requires equipment that does not depend upon room darkening.* (Photograph courtesy of Chabot College Library, Hayward, California.)

that the audiovisual collection be kept in closed storage in specialized cabinets and racks, or in a room removed from the book collection. Such an arrangement permits the use either of an accession number system or of the same subject classification used for books. Since access to material is by request only an up-to-date union and/or separate catalog must be maintained. Contingent factors in decision here are circulation policies, growth of the collection and the facilities, and future possibility of integration of materials.

UNION CATALOG

The integrated or union card or book catalog brings together in one place all resources of every type, under an organized system and uniform subject headings.

FIGURE 17. LIGHTWEIGHT FILMSTRIP PROJECTOR. *This type of equipment, lightweight and compact, is suitable for circulation.* (Photograph courtesy of Jefferson Elementary School District, Daly City, California.)

This complete information on available resources enables the user to determine easily and quickly what materials might be most useful for the required problem solution. It provides a choice of materials and the possibility of substitution should the desired items be already in use. Such a catalog may also suggest new ideas for varied approaches to a subject by employing different kinds of media.

According to local conditions and physical facilities, the library may be faced with the problem of maintaining two catalogs: a union catalog and an audiovisual catalog. If the nonbook materials collection is housed at a distance from the main catalog, a separate audiovisual catalog should be available at that location in addition to the main catalog.

The advantages of the union catalog are easily identified. However, each multi-media library should evaluate these advantages in the light of the frequency of use of the union catalog, storage facilities, and the expense of duplicate card production and personnel time needed to keep two catalogs up-to-date.

CLASSIFICATION SYSTEMS

Two types of classification systems are currently used by the majority of libraries for organizing audiovisual materials. These are an accession number and a subject classification (Dewey Decimal or Library of Congress) system. The need for a subject classification approach will determine which system will be adopted. If a subject arrangement of materials is desired the Dewey system should be employed. Otherwise an accession number system will suffice.

ACCESSION NUMBER SYSTEM

The accession number system uses a number that records the chronological order in which that particular item was added to the library collection (see exam-

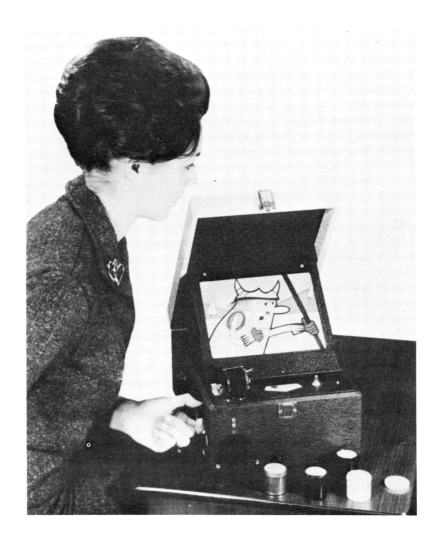

FIGURE 18. 35MM FILMSTRIP PROJECTOR. *Projectors are now being produced that emphasize compactness and light weight.* (Photograph courtesy of Viewlex, Inc.)

ples in Part 2). An accessioning record may be kept in an accession book similar to that utilized for books, or simply by indicating on a list of consecutive numbers the last one assigned. If an accession book is not maintained a record of withdrawals, lost items, additions, and other necessary information may be kept on a shelf list.

Accessioning material chronologically as it is received provides a running number count of all items and allows for unlimited expansion of the collection. An alternate method is to assign blocks of numbers to each kind of resource, e.g., 50,000 to 59,999 to filmstrips, 60,000 to 69,999 to recordings. The ultimate size of the collection of a particular type of material should be estimated so that the block of numbers allotted will take care of future growth. This system provides a mnemonic feature and places materials of the same kind in closer sequence for shelving.

The chief advantage of the accession number system is the simplicity of assigning call numbers. This simple routine task involves no judgment and saves professional time. Materials may be immediately available for use before full cataloging is completed.

On the other hand, problems are encountered in maintaining the correct numbering system and in devising a method to handle duplicate copies. If these are to be kept together the appropriate copy number is added to the accession number of the first acquisition, e.g., 3142 c.2. The running number count cannot then be used for inventory purposes. Since chronological numbering shows no relationship between number and subject the accession number system depends entirely on the use of a catalog to locate specific items by subject. It establishes completely separate storage of printed and audiovisual materials. Integration in the future would require reclassification of the entire collection entailing the replacement of all labels and catalog cards.

DEWEY DECIMAL CLASSIFICATION SYSTEM

Throughout the United States, although large libraries use the Library of Congress classification system, the majority of libraries employ the Dewey Decimal system. The same strengths and weaknesses of this classification method in organizing printed material appear when applied to nonbook materials.

Through the Dewey Decimal system audiovisual materials are classified by subject, and the integration and coordination of all resources is achieved. The Dewey classification number permits both print and non-print items to be shelved in the same manner, either together or separately, whichever seems most advantageous and best suited to local facilities. Future integration in shelving is provided for and the searcher is permitted to browse and gain valuable suggestions for substitutions and multi-media resources.

One of the chief problems found in this application of the Dewey system is the lack of subdivisions for forms of audiovisual materials. The addition of a letter symbol may solve this problem. Libraries with a large collection in a special subject (e.g., music or art) may find it advisable to devise a classification code specifically for the forms of this subject. Since the assigning of Dewey classification numbers is a professional task, the rate at which materials are made available for use will depend upon the amount of professional time provided for this service.

6

CATALOGING-COMMUNICATION WITH THE PATRON

Cataloging of nonbook materials, a major essential in their organization for use in all libraries, may sometimes loom as an insurmountable task. When confronted with an array of audiovisual resources, those who are unfamiliar with them may feel defeated by the very thought of researching and then devising their own cataloging systems. Therefore the intent of the information provided here is to furnish a useable general guide that will clarify and simplify cataloging procedures. There is no attempt to establish authoritarian cataloging rules which must be followed. Rather, the aim is to suggest methods based on accepted standard library practices, which are flexible enough to allow adaptation to the individual library or cataloging agency. In deciding the content and procedures to be included the following basic assumptions were made:

Print and nonprint materials will be made available through the same service agency, a library.

Personnel already familiar with the cataloging of printed materials will use this as a guide.

There will be adaptations determined by the local situation, relating especially to the facility that provides the cataloging service (which may be a school district, regional, county, or cooperative processing center, a commercial cataloger, or a single library), and the age, education, and literacy level of the people served by the library. Materials added to the children's collection of a public library or to an elementary school library may be cataloged in less detail than are those destined for an adult collection or a high school or college library.

Materials will not be limited only to those suitable for group presentation, but will be supplied for the use of the individual.

SYMBOLS AND COLOR CODES

The varying publics of traditional libraries assume that holdings described on catalog cards refer primarily to books. The realization that knowledge recorded in many formats is now available in the modern library may be a novel experience. Thus information on the catalog card must describe for the user the particular type of resource if it is other than a book. The identification of different forms of material may be accomplished in several ways:

A letter symbol may be placed above the classification (or accession) number (see the discussion of classification systems in the previous chapter).

Instead of a symbol the complete name of the material may be typed above the classification number, e.g., Transparency, Study Print. Even though this method may cause spacing problems and clutter on the card some librarians feel that it minimizes the searcher's confusion. This type of identification is currently being used by some commercial cataloging services.

The medium may be specified on the catalog card after the title, e.g., Filmstrip, Picture, Flash card. This specification may be eliminated if identification is made by the name of the material over the classification number.

Colored catalog cards, or color-banded cards, or a combination of both, may be used to indicate different media. Libraries may wish to employ only the symbol (or name), or both the symbol and the color code. For quick reference these should be posted on the card catalog in a prominent position.

Because there are several major problems associated with color coding, the current trend is to dispense with it. If a color code is used for catalog cards, the same colors must be carried through for circulation cards. To provide both these cards in color is an added expense in materials and time, and it becomes increasingly difficult to procure enough different colors to cover the rapidly expanding variety of nonbook resources. Libraries often have to make their own color banded cards, either by using a printing process, if adequate equipment is available, or by stripping the upper edge of the card with a color felt pen. The multiplicity of colors in itself can become confusing to the user as different types of materials are added to the collection. Many libraries limit the number of colors by assigning them only on the basis of medium of reproduction, e.g., all projected materials—films, filmstrips, slides, transparencies—are cataloged on blue cards; all audio materials—records, tapes—are color coded cherry. If colored cards are already in use for other purposes, e.g., to designate lost books, reference books, special collections, location of books on certain subjects, care must be taken to avoid duplication of these colors for identifying audiovisual items. Further limiting of colors can be achieved by using only one color, e.g., green, for all nonbook materials. However, if the library uses centralized or commercial cataloging, colored cards

TABLE 2. SYMBOLS AND COLOR CODES

MEDIUM	CATALOG CARD COLOR	SYMBOL
Art Print	Salmon	PA
Chart	Salmon	PC
Diorama	Brown strip	DD
Equipment	Gray strip	EQ*
Film	See Motion Picture Film	
Filmstrip	Green	FS
Flash Card	Salmon	PS
Game	Black strip	KL
Globe	Brown strip	DM
Kinescope	Blue	MP
Kit	Black strip	KT
Map	Salmon	PC
Microcard	Salmon	PM
Microfiche	Green	FF
Microfilm	Green	FM
Microprint	Salmon	PM
Mock-up, Model	Brown strip	DM
Motion Picture Film—16mm.	Blue	MP
Motion Picture Film—8mm.	Blue	ML
Picture	Salmon	PP*
Programmed Instruction	Black strip	KP
Realia	Brown strip	DS
Recording, disc	Cherry	RD
Slide	Buff	TS
Specimen	Brown strip	DS
Study Print	Salmon	PS
Tape Recording	Cherry	RT
Transparency	Buff	TR
Vertical File Material	Pink strip	VF*
Video Tape	Blue	MV

* Except for those marked with an asterisk, all symbols for identification of different media are from *Standards for Cataloging, Coding and Scheduling Educational Media* (Washington, D.C.: NEA, Department of Audiovisual Instruction, 1968). The use of these symbols is strongly recommended to encourage the establishment of standards that permit the integrated cataloging of all media. It is evident from the rapid progress in the computerizing of knowledge that all libraries must be increasingly concerned with the effects of automation on their procedures. To devise any system or adopt any code now without seriously considering its compatibility to computer technology is to invite future cataloging conversion problems.

are extremely impractical because they are not generally provided by these services.

Aside from these practical considerations, the continuance of color coding negates one of the basic objectives in the concept of the multi-media library, i.e., the complete integration of all forms of knowledge carriers. Color coding perpetuates the idea that audiovisual materials need not be regarded as an integral part of the library collection because it specifically separates them from books.

In spite of these problems, however, many librarians feel that color coding serves a useful purpose in their own local situation. For instance, children at the primary reading level often have more difficulty in identifying the type of material through the printed word than through color. The physical facilities and shelving arrangement may necessitate the use of color coding as a locator device, or the clientele may request it as a means for rapid identification of audiovisual materials. Each library will have to assess the value of color coding to its particular public, and decide whether or not the use of the letter symbol, or name alone, is sufficient for identification.

If color coding by type of media is desired, the color code suggested here may be used. It is recommended that all libraries within a large administrative unit, e.g., a school district, a public or county library, use the same symbols and the same color code.

PRINTED CARDS

Nonbook materials require more descriptive information on the catalog card than do books since both the nature of the material itself and storage facilities may limit their accessibility for user examination. It is therefore recommended that printed catalog cards be purchased if possible. The amount of revision on these cards should be kept to a minimum.

At present the Library of Congress is the main source of supply for card sets for phonorecords, films, and filmstrips. However, because of the rapid acquisition of all types of media in library collections, some of the major producers have had their audiovisual materials cataloged. Kits which include a full set of catalog cards, circulation cards, and labels can now be requested when items are ordered. Commercial cataloging firms also are increasing their scope to provide cataloging and processing kits for a variety of nonbook resources. Usually their cataloging is based on the 1967 *Anglo-American Cataloging Rules*, with classification numbers from the Ninth Abridged Edition of *Dewey Decimal Classification*, and subject headings from the Ninth Edition of *Sears List of Subject Headings*. Current purchase prices for kits range from $.25 to $1.25. The alert librarian should check availability of these kits from producers and commercial catalogers and evaluate what advantages in cost and service to patrons may result from their use. (See "Sources for Cataloging and Processing Kits for Audiovisual Kits" at the end of this chapter.)

ORDERING LIBRARY OF CONGRESS CARDS

To provide better and faster service the Library of Congress Card Division is now utilizing optical scanning machinery to read orders for catalog cards. This has necessitated the issue of a new order form designed specifically for optical scanning. Previously, forms of different colors and formats were needed to request cards for media other than books. Now, however, the same optical form serves for books, films, filmstrips, and recordings. The Library of Congress Card Division provides, free of charge, a three-month supply of these forms preprinted with the subscriber's account number and other pertinent information. Libraries may use their own single or multi-part optical forms if they have been designed to meet detailed specifications and are approved by the Card Division. Information on design and quality standards for optically read forms is available from the Library of Congress Card Division (Building 159, Navy Yard Annex, Washington, D.C. 20504).

Complete information on how to order Library of Congress cards accompanies the new optical forms. This detail should be carefully studied so that all instructions are followed correctly. Reproduced here are excerpts on how to order cards for nonbook media, how to order by card number and by author and title (composer and title, or title only) when the card number is not known.

HOW TO ORDER SPECIAL TYPES OF CARDS

"The optical forms distributed by the Card Division may be used for ordering all types of cards, including cards for filmstrips, motion pictures, and phonorecords. In each case, complete bibliographic information should be given, including author, title, place, publisher, date, edition, and series. For filmstrip, motion picture, phonorecord and annotated card orders:

1. Use the author line for composers or editors of recorded music.
2. Use the publisher line for producers of films and manufacturers of records.
3. Use the line immediately beneath the title line for the manufacturer's prefix letter(s), manufacturer's record number, and RPM of records.
4. If the card number is not known, indicate a filmstrip, motion picture, or phonorecord order by typing or printing Fil, Mp, or R, respectively, in the box labeled "L.C. Prefix" on the top line of the form." (From *Order Forms*. Library of Congress, 1968, p. 7)

The main source for card numbers for motion pictures, filmstrips and records, is the *National Union Catalog: Motion Pictures and Filmstrips*, and the *National Union Catalog: Music and Phonorecords* (see Services of Cataloging Information, this chapter). However, since these are quarterly, semi-annual, annual, or quinquennial cumulations, unless the production date of the material is known, the securing of card numbers could become a costly, time-consuming, and frustrating experience. Special care should be taken when copying card numbers from these publications. Very often motion pictures and filmstrips, and/or several filmstrips from different producers, may have identical titles. Therefore, before noting, the number, the title, type of material, and the producer should be carefully checked to ascertain that the correct cards are being ordered for the material on hand.

Library of Congress card number information may also be procured from some producers (Jam Handy, Long Filmslide, Popular Science for Filmstrip-of-the-Month, Society for Visual Education) who provide a listing of all their cataloged filmstrips with L.C. card numbers and suggested Dewey classification numbers.

HOW TO ORDER BY CARD NUMBER

"Ordering by card number is the most satisfactory method, provided that the numbers can be obtained with a minimum of searching. These card numbers can be obtained from book trade catalogs, current book lists and bibliographies and on the verso of the title page of many books. Along with the card number, also indicate the name of the author and the first word of the title as a means of verification in case of error." (From *Order Forms*. Library of Congress, 1968, pp. 6–7)

If the L.C. card number cannot be supplied, cards may be ordered at slightly greater cost by providing the title and other information requested on the card order slip. However, without the L.C. card number, there is no assurance that the material has been cataloged by the Library of Congress, since their cataloging of nonbook materials is not as comprehensive as their cataloging of books.

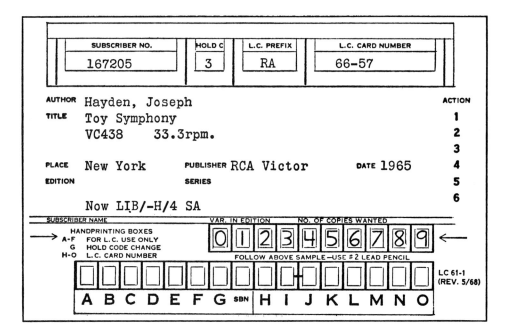

FORM 11. OPTICAL CARD ORDER FORM SUPPLIED BY THE
         LIBRARY OF CONGRESS. CATALOG CARDS
         FOR A RECORD

HOW TO ORDER BY AUTHOR AND TITLE

"Give the author's name in full, writing surname first, then forename and middle name or initial. The title of the book may be shortened, but the first word (except articles) should never be omitted. Abbreviate the place and the publisher. Never omit the date; if no date is given, write n.d. If the edition is other than the first, indicate this on the order form. If the publication is in a series, be sure to include a series note. A service charge of five cents is assessed for each author/title order." (From *Order Forms*. Library of Congress, 1968. p. 7)

(The illustration on page 51 shows how to order L.C. cards, for a filmstrip, by title. The optical L.C. card order form designed as the first slip of a multiple-copy book order form is used.)

Whether cards are ordered by number or by title, no delivery date is guaranteed. Receipt of cards may be expected anywhere from six weeks to well over a year after the order is placed. With the new optical scanning procedures, however, delivery of cards should become progressively more prompt. Since the *National Union Catalogs* reproduce the Library of Congress card and suggest a Dewey classification number for many films and filmstrips (not for phono-records), call numbers may be assigned, materials processed for circulation, and a temporary card filed in the card catalog. If cards are not readily obtainable from the Library of Congress, enlarged 3x5 reproductions of the *National Union Catalog* entries may be made if photo-duplication equipment is available.

For instructions on and examples of revision of L.C. cards, see Part 2.

GENERAL PRINCIPLES OF CATALOGING

Materials which differ in format and mode of reproduction require adaptations of standard library cataloging practices. Each departure from the general rule (as stated in the *Anglo-American Cataloging Rules*) and the amount of descriptive information included on the catalog card has been determined by the following considerations:

The integrated organization of printed and audiovisual materials extends the experiences and reinforces the skills already acquired by the library community.

The purpose of the catalog is to enable the user to determine easily all types of materials which might be useful in a given situation.

The catalog will be used by individuals within a wide age range, and of diverse, educational and ethnic backgrounds.

The call number and the catalog card form should be kept as simple as possible.

The vocabulary of description should be uninvolved and of an appropriate level of difficulty.

The minimum number of catalog cards to serve the purpose should be made.

Provision should be made for expansion as the materials collection grows.

The possibility of automated cataloging in the future should be kept in mind in determining main entry and items of information included on the card.

The same general principles that guide the degree of descriptive cataloging determined for books apply to the cataloging of nonbook materials. However, because of the physical format of these materials and the variety of storage facilities, it may be difficult to examine them. Therefore, the description on the card should be precise and definite, and full enough to inform the searcher that this may be the material he desires. Conversely, the description should not be so complete and lengthy as to be confusing.

Since the essential purpose of the catalog is to assist the user in determining and locating the available items which will best answer his needs, decisions as to how much information should be included on the catalog card will vary according to the local conditions and the particularities of the patrons of each library. Some of the basic considerations for judgment are:

AGE AND EDUCATION RANGE OF LIBRARY CLIENTELE Detailed source information and a sophisticated language of description may be intelligible to a scholar or educated adult but will only cause confusion and frustration for children and for those experiencing reading difficulties.

INTERESTS OF LIBRARY CLIENTELE More complete descriptive notes may be needed where there is particular demand for certain subjects, e.g., sociology. Where community activities or school curricula in art, music or dramatic arts are fully developed, it may be necessary to include more names of producers, performers, and artists.

CIRCULATION POLICIES   Restrictions on circulation and closed storage will require more detailed cataloging.

COSTS   The cost of professional and clerical time necessary for full descriptive cataloging should be realistically evaluated. In many instances, the use of funds for elaborate cataloging should be weighed against the possible use of funds to provide additional materials and services.

BASIC CATALOGING RULES AND ADAPTATIONS FOR NONBOOK MATERIALS

In order to provide full information for the same material under various entries, the Unit Card System is used. This consists of a basic unit card and duplicate cards with added entries, as shown in the tracings, placed above the main entry. Since these cards may involve a great deal of typing it is advisable to investigate various methods of card reproduction that might be available locally, such as mimeographing, multilithing, Xerography, photo duplication.

Since cataloging nonbook materials requires variations according to the kind of media, it is recommended that items be separated by type and all of one kind cataloged together. It is also time-saving to further divide each type of material by producer, since information needed for cataloging must often be obtained from their catalogs. Both book and nonbook materials are, however, cataloged according to the same basic rules: there are certain essential items of information which should be stated on the unit catalog card regardless of the kind of material being cataloged. For nonbook materials, this necessitates adaptations, which are made as follows:

CALL NUMBER   The call number is composed of: (1) A symbol of capital letters to designate type of material (see Symbols and Color Codes), or the name of the material; (2) a number, either an accession or classification number from Dewey or Library of Congress, placed under the material symbol.

According to the practice of the library, no letter, one, two or three letters, or letters and a Cutter number, may be placed below the classification number. These letters are derived from the beginning filing word (disregard a, an, the) of the main entry, e.g., *FS 539 At* would be the call number for a filmstrip entitled *The atom.* These letters are not needed if the accession number system is used.

MAIN ENTRY   Use *title main entry* for all nonbook materials. If the material (e.g., recording of several different selections) has no specific title, the cataloger may supply a conventional or filing title which will serve as a unifying and identifying element. Recordings of musical works whose titles are non-distinctive in that they essentially denote the form of composition should be entered under a title using the possessive form of the composer's name as the first word of the title, e.g., *Beethoven's Symphony No. 6 in F major, Mendelssohn's Violin Concerto in E minor.*

This form should also be used for recordings and art prints with distinctive titles if the library wishes to keep together all the works of each composer, author and/or artist. Thus the title main entry for *Richard III* becomes *Shakespeare's Richard III.* Added entries are made for the title of the work and for the author's full name.

The advantages of title main entry are numerous. The busy librarian who devotes the major portion of her time to working with individuals and groups cannot find the hours necessary for searching out various rules for main entry which differ for each type of material. Nor can she be expected to remember in detail the order of main entry preference for composers, performers, producers and other persons considered important. This is one of the tasks of the professional cataloger, who is at present in short supply and expensive to procure. For the practicing librarian, title main entry establishes simplicity of procedure and standardization. For the user of instructional resources it minimizes frustration since the majority of these materials are requested by title. For future growth of the collection and the possibility of automation in library procedures it provides a set-up that will adapt without difficulty to computer processing.

For recordings and art prints, an alternate main entry under the full name of the person responsible for the work may be used (see *Anglo-American Cataloging Rules*) if this is judged to be more helpful to the searcher.

IDENTIFICATION OF MATERIAL Identification of the type of material follows the title, using the singular form of the descriptive word, as filmstrip; record (or recording), disc, phonodisc, or audiodisc; record (or recording), tape, phonotape, or audiotape; slide; specimen (see Part 2).

ADDITIONAL TITLE INFORMATION Further clarification of the form of the material which is directly related to the title follows the identification of material. For example: Adapted from the book by Charles Dickens; Songs with guitar accompaniment; Narrated and sung by Bing Crosby. This information is not repeated in a note.

IMPRINT Name of the producer or manufacturer. An abbreviated form may be used if the abbreviation is such that the name of the company is recognized easily. For example, RCA may be known to the public, but CRG, Children's Record Guild, or YLP, Your Lesson Plan Materials, may be puzzling. A list of producer abbreviations may be found in the various sources of cataloging information at the end of this chapter. It is helpful to keep an up-to-date card file of abbreviations used. These should conform to those recorded on the producer's card in the Acquisition Quick-Reference File.

The latest copyright date follows the name of the producer. The use of "c" for copyright, and of square brackets to show that the date was obtained from other sources, is optional according to the practices of the library, as is the notation "n.d." when no date can be found.

COLLATION The physical description of the material includes the form of reproduction, the length of time or amount of information included, and any necessary dimensions which will indicate to the user the type of equipment needed for reproduction. Use the following abbreviations for physical description:

b&w	black and white
ea.	each
fps.	frames per second (motion picture speed)
Guide	teacher's manual or study guide
"	inches (disc recording diameter)
ips.	inches-per-second (tape recordings)
min.	minutes (running time)
mono	monaural (disc and tape recordings)
mm	millimeter (width)
rpm.	revolutions-per-minute (disc recordings)
s.	sides (disc recordings)
sd.	sound
si.	silent
stereo	stereophonic (disc and tape recordings)

SERIES NOTE   If a unit in a set or series is cataloged separately, note the title of the series. This may be followed by the number of the unit in the series if it is necessary for identification, e.g., Earth, home of man #4. The use of parentheses around the series note is optional.

While it is not essential that the series note be included as part of the basic information on the catalog card, it has been found that many patrons, especially teachers and personnel in education, are acquainted with materials by series titles, which often indicate broad subject areas in which they are interested. Series notes also facilitate ordering since producers' catalogs often index materials primarily by series, with individual items either in a second index or not listed at all.

GRADE LEVEL   Designation of grade level will be used most frequently in a school situation. If grade level suitability is customarily given, and disproportionate, time-consuming research is not needed to ascertain it, use specific numbers (e.g., K–3, 4–6, 5–7, 7–9) or word indications abbreviated as follows:

K	Kindergarten
P	Primary grades (K–3)
El, or, I	Elementary or intermediate grades (4–6)
JH, or, J	Junior high school
HS, or, S	Senior high school (9–12 or 10–12)
C, or, A	College or university
Ad	Adult

ACCOMPANYING MATERIAL   Complete communication of ideas may necessitate reinforcement of one type of material by other media. Producers have specifically designed these to be used together as accompanying materials. Care should be taken to ascertain that the items under consideration are intended to accompany each other and are not separate entities packaged together for commercial purposes only. For example, a filmstrip, a record, and a book, each produced by a different publisher, though advertised or combined by a vendor as accompanying material, may not be synchronized even though they are on the same subject. If desired, the items may be cataloged separately, or as a kit.

In order to draw together all parts of an audiovisual unit, note any accompanying material (e.g., teaching guide, printed text, descriptive notes, etc.) and a physical description of it if needed (e.g., record, disc: 2s, 10", 78rpm; filmstrip: 37fr., color, 35mm). *This will have the same call number (including type of ma-*

terial symbol) as the material it accompanies. Thus a recording may bear a film-strip symbol, or vice versa. For example, a disc recording which accompanies a filmstrip on science will be labeled with the same symbol in the call number as the filmstrip, e.g., FS 500 Sc. Similarly, a filmstrip which is correlated with a disc recording of folk songs will be labeled with the same symbol in the call number as the recording, e.g., RD 784 Fo. *Where the call number is the same it is not necessary to repeat it after the statement of accompanying material.*

If the call number and/or title differ from those of the material they accom-pany, *they should be recorded* after the statement and description of the accom-panying material. Different call numbers and titles may often occur. For example, one teaching guide may relate to all the filmstrips in a series where each individual filmstrip has a different call number and title. The teaching guide will carry the call number and title of filmstrip no. 1. This call number and title must be noted on the catalog card for filmstrip no. 2 and all the other filmstrips in the series to properly identify the materials which correlate with them also. In this way, the library user will be sure to get all the necessary components of the unit requested.

Where two or more filmstrips are synchronized with one disc or tape record-ing (e.g., each side of a recording relates to a different filmstrip), the filmstrips should be cataloged as a set under the call number and title of filmstrip no. 1. The recording, bearing the same call number and title as filmstrip no. 1, is noted as accompanying material. Title added entries are made for the other filmstrips.

NOTES   A contents note is used if the material includes several different items or selections from various sources. The importance of listing the contents remains a matter of judgment. One side of a recording may contain ten or more primary songs whose exact titles may be of little interest to the library user. Conversely, noting which *Just So Stories* are narrated on a record would be helpful to the per-son seeking Kipling's stories. Extensive contents notes often necessitate continua-tion cards. These should be kept to a minimum since they are confusing both for the personnel who file the cards and those who use them.

A brief summary may be added. Wherever possible, it should suggest rela-tionships of the material to known interests of the user. In a school media center, for example, a curriculum-oriented resume may be of assistance to both teachers and students.

ADDED ENTRIES   Subject—Follow the practices of the library in assigning subject headings to books, using the same subject heading source, with additions as necessary.

Composer or Author—Entries may be needed where main entry could have been made under his name instead of under title, or where the material is an adaptation of a work of a well-known author.

Performer or Narrator—Entries are needed only where names are well known and popular enough that information is likely to be sought under the name.

Series—If each unit of the series has been cataloged separately, a composite series card may be made listing the various items in the series, either by number or alphabetically by title, instead of using the unit card with a series added entry. In-formation stated on the series card includes the title of the series, identification of material, producer, date, and call number and title of each unit in the series.

TITLE ANALYTICS   Make for each unit of a series or set if the set is cata-loged as a whole and the title of each unit differs from that of the set. Also for important titles listed in the contents note.

TRACINGS   Make tracings on the main entry or shelf list card in the following order: subject headings listed alphabetically; author, composer, narrator, performer, or other important names, alphabetically by surname; series; title analytics in alphabetical sequence.

SHELF LIST CARD   In order to provide space on the shelf list card for acquisition information, the notes appearing after the statement of accompanying material may be omitted from the unit card. Enter instead the producer's catalog number, source, price and date of acquisition.

THE CIRCULATION CARD   In order to minimize confusion and error in matching checkout cards to material, include the following information on the circulation card: call number; copy or accession number; title; producer and/or producer's catalog number (optional—useful for quick identification where titles are similar); number of items if more than one; statement of accompanying material (see below).

Statement of accompanying material on circulation card.

Complications can arise in the checkout of accompanying material which is often stored separately and/or correlates with several different items. The following general rules will simplify circulation procedures, and may be adapted as necessary.

> The accompanying material correlates only with the parent item, has the same call number and title, and is stored with it: on circulation card of parent item type statement of accompanying material prefixed by w/, e.g., w/guide.
>
> The accompanying material correlates only with the parent item, has the same call number and title, but is stored separately. On circulation card of parent item *enclose in parentheses* the statement of accompanying material. This informs both the user and circulation personnel that the material is available but is not checked out on that circulation card.
>
> Make a separate circulation card for the accompanying material. Include a statement to identify kind of material, e.g., Record, disc.
>
> The accompanying material correlates with several different items, has a different call number and/or title, and is stored separately: on circulation card of parent item *enclose in parentheses* the statement of accompanying material, *followed by its title and call number*. This informs both the user and circulation personnel that the material is available, that *it has its own circulation card which is filed under the title or call number noted*.

Circulation cross reference cards.

When several items with different titles are synchronized with one recording, they are cataloged as a unit under one title and one call number, and are checked out on one circulation card. A circulation file cross reference card (preferably of a different color than the circulation cards) may be made from the added entry titles to the main entry title so that library personnel can quickly locate the applicable circulation card. Include call number of main entry on cross reference card.

POCKET FOR CIRCULATION CARD   The affixing of a pocket to hold the circulation card is limited by the physical format of nonbook materials. If a pocket is made, it should show the same information as the circulation card, except that the statement of accompanying material may be omitted.

TYPING FORMAT

Apply the rules used for typing catalog cards for books, following local practice with regard to indention spacing, first line used on the card, punctuation and spacing after punctuation, and capitalization. Fewer continuation cards will be needed if elite type is used.

Form of the Card:

The hanging indention form is used where the main entry for nonbook materials is under title. The conventional form of *author main entry* for books is followed if the composer or artist is chosen as the main entry for recordings and/or art prints.

```
          12345678901234567890
          2              SUBJECT HEADING or other added entry . . . .
call      3  SYMBOL       . . . . . . . . . . . . . . . . . . . .
num-      4  Class# Title.  Identification of material.  Subtitle
ber       5  Letters   or additional information.   Producer, date.
          6              Physical description: form, time, size.
          7            Series.  Grade level.
          8            Accompanying material.
          9
          10             Contents note . . . . . . . . . . . . . . .
          11         . . . . . . . . . . . . . . . . . . . . . . .
          12             Annotation or summary . . . . . . . . . . .
          13         . . . . . . . . . . . . . . . . . . . . . . .
          14
          15         Tracings
          16
          17
```

FORM 12. FORMAT FOR CATALOG CARDS

The unit card form shown above is used for all sample cards in this book. Typing and spacing rules for this form are:

INDENTION

The first indention is 10 spaces from the edge of the card: begin on space 11. The second indention is 13 spaces from the edge: begin on space 14. The third indention is 16 spaces from the edge: begin on space 17.

CALL NUMBER   Begin one space from edge, on third line; capitalize symbols for type of material.

TITLE MAIN ENTRY   On fourth line begin at first indention. Begin all subsequent lines at the second indention until the second line of the series, contents note, or summary is reached, which begins at the *first* indention.

IDENTIFICATION OF MATERIAL   Begin two spaces after end of title.

SUBTITLE, ETC.   Begin two spaces after end of identification of material.

IMPRINT   Begin three spaces after subtitle, or after material identification if subtitle, etc., is omitted.

COLLATION   Begin at second indention, on next line.

SERIES NOTE   Begin three spaces after collation. Parentheses around series note are optional.

GRADE LEVEL   Begin three spaces after series note, or after collation if there is no series note, followed by a period. Indication of grade level is optional.

ACCOMPANYING MATERIAL   On next line, begin at second indention. A colon is placed after the statement of accompanying material if designation of title and call number, and/or physical description, is necessary. Where several items are listed they are separated by a semi-colon and capitalization of the initial letter of the next item.

CONTENTS NOTE   Skip a line, begin at second indention, starting subsequent lines at first indention.

SUMMARY   On next line, begin at second indention, starting subsequent lines at first indention.

CONTINUATION CARD   If a continuation card is needed, type "cont'd on next card" to the right of the guard hole. In the upper right corner of the second card, on the first line, type "Card 2." Type call number and title main entry only on fourth line. Skip a line and continue contents note beginning at first indention, starting subsequent lines at first indention.

ADDED ENTRIES   Capitalize all letters of a subject heading. Begin all added entries on the second line at the second indention, starting subsequent lines at the third indention.

TRACINGS   All subject tracings are typed in capitals. Use a slash mark to separate entries. If title analytics are made for every title listed in the contents note the designation "t" is sufficient. However, if cards are made for only some of the titles, these should be given after the designation "t" followed by a colon. Use the abbreviation "ser" for series.

SERIES CARD   Begin series title on second line at second indention. Two spaces after, type the identification of material. Another three spaces, note publisher and date. If information extends to the next line, begin at third indention. Begin listing individual items on fourth line using a separate line for each. Type the class number one space from the edge of the card, space two, and add the letters of the call number. Material identification symbols are not needed. Start the title of the unit at the third indention.

CATALOG CARD REPRODUCTION

The description of nonbook material on a catalog card requires a considerable amount of typing. This often holds true even for very simplified cataloging. If a library prepares its own catalog cards it should attempt to find reproduction techniques to relieve the burden of typing one very full catalog card four to six times to provide a complete set of cards for only one acquisition. Satisfactory cards can be produced by several different copying methods. Depending upon the volume of cards needed, the size of the library or of the cataloging facility, and the availability of equipment, these may range from an offset press to a small hand operated card mimeograph. If the library has the use of a Xerox 914, clear and legible duplicate catalog cards can be made quickly and inexpensively. By using a very simple template six cards for six different titles may be held in place and reproduced in one printing on six-up card stock available from the major library supply firms. The typist then need only type in the appropriate headings. The Xerox representative should be consulted for detailed instructions on how to set the machine for card reproduction. If the library cannot handle its own cards, the Xerox Company offers a commercial duplicating service that reproduces cards in any quantity requested.

SOURCES FOR CATALOGING
AND PROCESSING KITS
FOR AUDIOVISUAL MATERIALS

Bro-Dart, Inc. Instructional Media Department, P.O. Box 923, 1609 Memorial Ave., Williamsport, Pa. 17701.

Audiovisual materials are cataloged by Alanar, Bro-Dart's custom cataloging division. The company supplies kits for Spoken Word and Caedmon recordings, the productions of Jam Handy, Enrichment Teaching Materials, and the Encyclopaedia Britannica Educational Corporation, and for titles appearing in the *Elementary School Library Collection*. All filmstrips in a series are included in one kit. Individual filmstrips in a series are not cataloged separately. Bro-Dart also produces book catalogs by contract.

National Information Center for Educational Media. University of Southern California, University Park, Los Angeles, Calif. 90007.

NICEM's card service is available to all types of libraries, for nonbook materials only. Libraries provide their own classification information. Catalog cards are printed on the computer.

Professional Library Service. 2200 E. McFadden Ave., Santa Ana, Calif. 92705, and, Library Journal Cards. 1180 Avenue of the Americas, New York, N.Y. 10036.

PLS has built up a computer bank of audiovisual resources through its book catalog service to several colleges and school districts. It does not sell kits directly to libraries. Through Library Journal Cards it supplies kits to producers and distributors who make them available to their customers. It catalogs the products of Coronet Films, Imperial Films, Tweedy Transparencies, and University Microfilms. The full media name instead of a symbol is used, and a single kit covers all titles in a series if they pertain to the same subject.

Specialized Service & Supply Co., Inc. (SSS). 1329 Arlington St., Cincinnati, Ohio 45225.

Stock kits for the collections of Bailey Films, Creative Visuals, Eye Gate House, McGraw-Hill Test-Films, Society for Visual Education, 3M (transparencies), and Western Publishing Company (transparencies and filmstrips). These may be procured from SSS or from the producer. The media name is printed above the call number. Each title in a series is cataloged individually.

Stone Bridge Press, Inc. Gilsum, N.H. 03448.

Provides kits for fourteen types of media produced by various companies. It is the only company that color codes its cards (six colors). Cards without color coding cost $.10 more per set. Symbols identify the media, and a separate kit is available for each title in a series.

Xlibra. P.O. Box 270, Portland, Ore. 97207.

Produces and markets kits for sixteen types of selected media cataloged by Northwest Library Service, Inc. (P.O. Box 25112, Portland, Ore. 97225) in accordance with their *Cataloging Standards for Non-Book Materials*. Classification is by accession number, with media symbols, and simplified cataloging is used.

SOURCES OF CATALOGING INFORMATION

Audio Cardalog. Max U. Bildersee. Box 989, Larchmont, N.Y. 10538. 10/yr.

Contains reviews, on cards, of selected disc and tape recordings, including annotations, physical descriptions, suggested subject heading, and evaluation.

Gaver, Mary V., ed. *The Elementary School Library Collection: A Guide to Books and Other Media. Phases 1–2–3.* 4th ed. and supplement. Newark: Bro-Dart, 1968.

Integrates audiovisual materials with related books, also listing them separately by Dewey classification.

NICEM Index to 16mm Educational Films, NICEM Index to 8mm Educational Motion Cartridges, NICEM Index to 35mm Educational Filmstrips, NICEM Index to Overhead Transparencies.

See "Buying Guides," Chapter 4 of this book, for description and full bibliographic data.

U.S. Library of Congress. *The National Union Catalog: Motion Pictures and Filmstrips.* Quarterly, with annual and quinquennial cumulations. New York: Rowman & Littlefield, 1953–57, 1958–62. Ann Arbor: J. W. Edwards, 1963–67. Washington, D.C.: Library of Congress, 1968–.

Reproduces Library of Congress catalog cards for 16mm and 8mm films, and for filmstrips.

U.S. Library of Congress. *The National Union Catalog: Music and Phonorecords.* Semi-annual, with annual and quinquennial cumulations. New York: Rowman &

Littlefield, 1953–57, 1958–62. Ann Arbor: J. W. Edwards, 1963–67. Washington, D.C.: Library of Congress, 1968–.

Reproduces Library of Congress catalog cards for disc recordings, and a few tapes.

See also periodicals that review audiovisual materials, discussed in Chapter 3, and producers' and vendors' catalogs. Additional sources of information about a specific type of material will be found in Part 2.

BIBLIOGRAPHY

American Library Association. *Anglo-American Cataloging Rules: North American Text.* Edited by C. Sumner Spalding. Chicago: A.L.A., 1967.

Badton, Jean, and Nancy Motomatzu. "Commercial Media Cataloging—What's Holding Us Up." *School Library Journal* 15, No. 3 (Nov. 1968): 34–35.

Barnes, Christopher. "Classification and Cataloging of Spoken Records in Academic Libraries." *College & Research Libraries* 28, No. 1 (Jan. 1967): 49–52.

Brown, Louis H. "Retrieving Media Information According to Content on Subject Area." *Audiovisual Instruction* 14, No. 2 (Feb. 1969): 71–74.

Carson, Doris M. "Cataloging Nonbook Materials." *Wilson Library Bulletin* 43 (Mar. 1965): 562–64.

Church Library Service. Baptist Sunday School Board. *Guide for Processing, Cataloging, and Circulating Audio-Visual Materials.* Nashville, Tenn.: Church Library Service, n.d.

Clarke, Virginia. *The Organization of Nonbook Materials in the Laboratory School Library, North Texas State University.* N. Texas State University, 1965.

Columbia University. School of Library Service. *Sample Catalog Cards for Use in Connection with Courses in Technical Services in Libraries and Organization of Materials.* 4th ed. New York: Columbia University, 1967.

Daily, Jay E. "The Selection, Processing, and Storage of Non-Print Materials: A Critique of the Anglo-American Cataloging Rules as They Relate to Newer Media," *Library Trends* 16, No. 2 (Oct. 1967): 283–89.

Doyle, Leila. "Central Processing." *The Instructor* 25, No. 3 (Nov. 1965): 67.

Dunkin, Paul S. *Cataloging U.S.A.* Chicago: A.L.A., 1969.

Egan, Mary J. "Tiptoe in Technology," *School Library Journal* 13, No. 8 (Apr. 1967): 49–51.

Geller, Evelyn. "Commercial Media Cataloging—What's Around?" *School Library Journal* 15, No. 3 (Nov. 1968): 27–33.

Gerletti, Robert C. "Digital Apoplexy: Certain Diagnosis, No Easy Cure." *School Library Journal* 15, No. 3 (Nov. 1968): 36–37.

Harris, Evelyn J. *Instructional Materials Cataloging Guide*. Tucson, Ariz.: University of Arizona, College of Education, 1968.

Hawken, William R. *Copying Methods Manual*. Chicago: A.L.A. Library Technology Program, 1966.

Hickey, Doralyn J. "Bridging the Gap between Cataloging and Information Retrieval." *Library Resources & Technical Services* 11, No. 2 (Spring 1967): 173–83.

Hicks, Warren B. and Alma M. Tillin. *The Organization of Nonbook Materials in School Libraries*. Sacramento, Calif.: State Dept. of Education, 1967.

Hogan, Dan E. "Let Your School Library Catalog Cut Across the Media." *School Library Journal* 11, No. 4 (Dec. 1964): 31–34.

Holdridge, R. E. "Cataloging Nonbook Materials," *Audiovisual Instruction* 12, No. 4 (Apr. 1967): 358.

Hopkinson, Shirley L. *The Descriptive Cataloging of Library Materials*. 3rd ed. San Jose, Calif.: Claremont House, 1968.

National Education Association. Department of Audiovisual Instruction. *Standards for Cataloging, Coding, and Scheduling Educational Media*. Washington, D.C.: N.E.A., 1968.

Nichols, H. L. *Guidelines to Audio-Visual Cataloging by Means of Data Processing.* Sacramento, Calif.: Bureau of Audiovisual and School Library Education, California State Dept. of Education, 1966.

Piercy, Esther J. *Commonsense Cataloging: A Manual for the Organization of Books and Other Materials in School and Small Public Libraries*. New York: H. W. Wilson, 1965.

Plunkett, Dalton G. and Allan D. Quick. *Cataloging Standards for Non-Book Materials: A Complete Guide to Cataloging Non-Book Materials in the Individual School*. Tigard, Ore.: Northwest Library Service, 1968.

Slocum, Robert B. and Lois Hacker. *Sample Cataloging Forms: Illustrations of Solutions to Problems in Descriptive Cataloging*. 2nd rev. ed. Metuchen, N.J.: Scarecrow Press, 1968.

Stoops, Betty. "Cataloging and Classification Systems for Instructional Materials." *Audiovisual Instruction* 9 (Sept. 1964): 427–28.

U.S. Library of Congress. Descriptive Cataloging Division. *Rules for Descriptive Cataloging in the Library of Congress: Motion Pictures and Filmstrips*. Washington, D.C., 1965.

U.S. Library of Congress. Descriptive Cataloging Division. *Rules for Descriptive Cataloging in the Library of Congress: Phonorecords.* 2nd preliminary ed. Washington, D.C., 1964.

Westhuis, Judith L. and Julia M. DeYoung. *Cataloging Manual for Nonbook Materials in Learning Centers and School Libraries.* Ann Arbor, Mich.: Michigan Association of School Librarians, 1966.

Westby, Barbara M. "Commercial Processing Firms: A Directory." *Library Resources & Technical Services* 13 (Spring 1969): 209–286.

Yesner, Bernice L. *Administering a Filmstrip Collection.* New York: McGraw-Hill, 1966.

7

PHYSICAL PROCESSING
AND STORAGE

DECISION FACTORS

Ingenuity on the part of the administrator is a valuable asset in the physical processing of nonbook materials. This phase in the organization of all types of media cannot be regulated by rigid rules. At present there is constant flux and experimentation in the commercial packaging and the contents of products, which demand a wide latitude in physical processing. The placement of labels, for example, may often have to be a matter of judgment rather than of rule, since it may be dictated by the size and shape of a container. How these heterogeneous items are fitted into existing storage facilities may necessitate on-the-spot determinations applicable only to certain specific items rather than to an entire genre. In essence, decisions on general procedures and supplies acquired for physical processing must implement the following objectives:

To provide a collection of materials organized for maximum availability and ease of access to the user.
To provide sufficient protection of materials to insure maximum circulation.
To provide sufficient information to facilitate circulation procedures and rehousing.
To provide for expansion.

Specifically, the formulation of physical processing procedures will be affected in each library by certain local conditions, such as:

Users of materials: socio-economic level of library community; adults and/or children; group and/or individual use.
Facilities for storage: amount and kind of shelving, cabinets, etc., available; housing of materials in separate quarters or with books.
Classification scheme and cataloging practices adopted for nonbook materials.
Circulation routines.

Delivery practices and shipping requirements.

Expense of processing materials as related to the amount and length of time material will be used.

Expense of clerical time involved in physical processing as related to the amount and length of time material will be used.

It is therefore feasible to accept as the guiding rule in physical processing of nonbook materials the statement that it is permissible to use whatever works to accomplish the greatest efficiency in preparation and the least frustration in patron use. Consequently, there is no attempt here to prescribe any definitive method of physical processing. Various procedures are suggested that may be of help when adapted to any specific local situation. Because of the great variety in size, shape, and specialized information needed, each type of material is treated separately in Part 2. Neither the local production of materials nor their maintenance and repair are included.

PROCEDURAL PATTERN

The steps in the physical processing of all types of nonbook materials follow the same general pattern.

Separate the various types of material so that all of one kind may be processed together.

Prepare a container or protective covering. Circulation procedures, users, and housing facilities, determine the weight, size, shape, material of the container (e.g., heavy string-tie or plastic envelope).

Mark ownership identification on each separate item and on container by any of the following methods: rubber stamping on material (e.g., on reverse of picture); rubber stamping or typing on label; perforating (e.g., leader of filmstrip); lettering (e.g., on equipment).

Prepare labels. The kind of media and the amount of information required determine the number of labels needed, their size, shape and type, and how much of the following information should be typed on them: ownership identification, call number, copy number, serial or identification number, total number of items in a set, number of each individual item in a set, title, subject, contents, inventory and/or picture or diagram showing layout of multiple items in one container. Labels may be self-adhesive (available in a variety of sizes and shapes), tie-on lightweight cardboard, or paper cut to size and pasted on.

Pressure sensitive, permanently adhesive labels in a wide variety of sizes, shapes and colors, are available from local and national label manufacturers. If the library were to stock labels in sizes and shapes tailored specifically to the packaging of each type of audiovisual material an exceedingly large proportion of the supplies budget would have to be encumbered in the initial outlay. As a rule, label suppliers quote prices ranging from $50 to $100 for the purchase of a minimum quantity of labels. Every change in size and/or shape entails the addition of another $50 to $100. It is therefore advisable to study very carefully the sizes and shapes of labels available and decide on one or two that will serve for the majority of nonbook items. In addition, they should be set up in a format that permits easy insertion into the typewriter and continuous straight-across typing of several labels in one operation.

Experience has shown that there are two sizes which perform best for multi-purpose labeling. For call numbers only, a ½" x ½" label (see Filmstrips, Part 2) is very satisfactory. For preprinted or stamped owner identification, with or without call number notation, a 1½" x 1" label fits on almost every type of material, including phonograph records (see sample, Recordings, disc, Part 2). The printing of the library name should not exceed ⅜" on the upper portion of the label, leaving ⅝" in which to type the call number. To facilitate typing, they should also be ordered in roll form with 4, 6, or 8-up. Larger or smaller labels for special containers (e.g., round labels for filmstrip can lids) or purposes, such as inventory or contents listing, are available in lesser quantities, on sheets, from library supply houses. The labels shown here may be procured from the Avery Label Company, which has offices in most of the large cities throughout the country, or from other national or local firms.

LINCOLN LIBRARY	LINCOLN LIBRARY
Learning Unified	Learning Unified
School District	School District
RD	RD
785	785
Da	Da c.2

FORM 13. MULTI-PURPOSE LABELS

Affix labels to material and container in a position which is uniform for each type of material and most visible when material is stored.

Check that each item in a set is labeled and identified by the number shown on the contents or inventory label.

Protect labels by applying Scotch tape, plastic spray, lacquer, white glue, or label protectors. White glue is highly recommended because it is easy to apply, dries clear in a few minutes, and has good adhesive quality (see Filmstrips, Part 2).

Paste on pocket if appropriate to circulation procedures and packaging. It should not be placed on the exterior of envelopes or containers where it will impede shelving and filing, and be quickly damaged.

If a separate date-due form is used and is necessary for circulation, adhere it with pocket inside container.

EQUIPMENT AND SUPPLIES

Continuous perusal of periodicals, current brochures and catalogs in the audiovisual field, will inform the alert librarian of the increasing availability of new equipment and supplies for physical processing. It will also stimulate original ideas which, if successfully worked out for a particular resource center may be passed on to others. The *ALA Bulletin*, in its regular department reports, "Library Technology" and "New Products" (formerly "Goods and Gadgets"), offers valuable suggestions. Since library supply houses now stock many supplies and varied equipment essential for processing and housing nonbook materials, the librarian may not have to look elsewhere to procure the basic items needed to begin physical processing. It is advisable to keep on file the latest catalogs and special announcements of the following major library suppliers: Bro–Dart, Inc. (56 Earl St., Newark, N.J. 07114); Demco (Box 1488, Madison, Wis. 53701; Box 1586, Fresno, Calif. 93716; Box 4231, Hamden, Conn. 06514); Gaylord Bros., Inc. (155 Gifford St., Syracuse, N.Y. 13201; 29 North Aurora St., Stockton, Calif. 95201); Library Bureau (122 E. 42nd St., New York, N.Y. 10017).

The equipment and supplies indicated here will facilitate physical processing. Not included are those that are found in most libraries for book treatment. The list is only suggestive, since many articles may be essential while others would be useful to have but could be deferred for later purchase.

EQUIPMENT

Dry mount press
Label printing machine
Laminating machine
Long-neck heavy duty stapler
Mounting iron
Pasting machine
Sorting racks
Splicers, 8mm and 16mm

SUPPLIES

Containers:
    Canvas, polyethylene bags
    Cardboard, fiberboard, steel boxes
    Plastic cans, one-piece lid attached, for filmstrips
    Large, red, string-tie, heavy manila, plastic envelopes
    Albums, sleeves, jackets, of plastic or pressboard, for records
    Special purpose containers for correlated materials.
Miscellaneous:
    Cardboard, corrugated
    Cleaning fluids and cloths
    Gummed butcher paper
    Labels, various sizes: self-adhering pressure sensitive; gummed; tie-on, light-weight cardboard
    Leader tape, head and tail
    Masking tape, various widths
    Write-on tape, self-adhering pressure sensitive
Mounting materials:
    Chipboard, no. 4
    Cover paper, 9"x12", 12"x18"

Dry mounting tissue
Mounting board, standard
Mounting paper, heavy
Picture hangers: "Braquette" style; Mul-T-Pic print holders
Rubber cement and thinner
Suspension eyelets
Spring rollers

INVENTORY AND REORDER

As with all library supplies, the periodic inventory and reorder of items always required for the physical processing of nonbook resources can become quite a lengthy and involved activity. A Supplies Order File has proven to be a very simple and efficient tool for minimizing the computations and specifications research needed to ensure the continuous provision of supplies. A separate card is used for each article. The information recorded on it includes the type of material, the date ordered and the Purchase Order number, the vendor, and the quantity, description and cost. Typing requisitions will be facilitated if this information is noted on the card in the same sequence as appears on the requisition.

A good estimate of the amount of material used in a period of time (monthly or quarterly) can be made by comparing the dates and quantities shown for previous orders. No further search in catalogs for numbers and detailed descriptions is needed since these also are on the card. Should it be necessary to consult

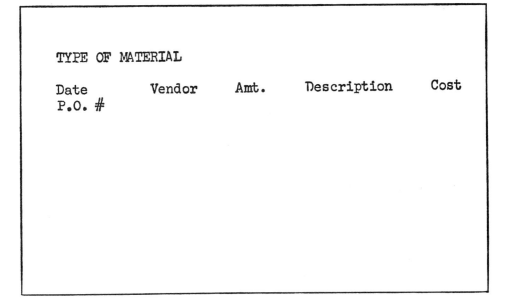

FORM 14. FORMAT OF CARD FOR SUPPLIES ORDER FILE

```
LABELS - IMPRINTED A-V

10/68  Avery Label Co.   1 lot   20,000 labels        90.20
P.O.# 71648                      1½"x1", imprinted/spec
                                 white label, black
                                 printings, DS 2416,
                                 MW4, LRO, P-4   4.51/M
10/69        "            1 lot          "            90.20
P.O.# 84232
```

FORM 15. CARD FOR SUPPLIES ORDER FILE

a prior Purchase Order, the number is immediately available. The benefits derived from a Supplies Order File far outweigh the cost of the small amount of time required to maintain it.

HOUSING ACCOMMODATIONS

Although the shelving and storage of audiovisual resources can generate problems, the library should not delay the acquisition of these materials until housing conditions are ideal. This is indeed an area that presents tremendous challenge and promotes full play of the imagination and creative talents. Libraries throughout the country are experimenting, and fabricating storage units which work in their own situations. Exchange of these ideas should be encouraged. If shop or manual training facilities are available they can also render invaluable assistance in carrying out plans.

Manufacturers are now offering a rapidly increasing quantity and variety of containers and cabinets specially designed to accommodate audiovisuals. These may be fitted into the library proper, or if necessary, set up in an adjacent space or in a room farther removed. Ideally, all types of media should be shelved together. Integrated storage presents for the patron's benefit the broad range of media available on any subject. Such integration, however, cannot be practiced to its fullest extent until modular containers and facilities are devised which will permit varied sizes and shapes to be placed with books on standard library shelving.

Surveyed here are various means of storage now on the market. They may be procured from library supplies and furniture firms, from producers of audio-

FIGURE 19. SHELVING FOR STORAGE OF AUDIOVISUAL MATE-
RIALS. (Photograph courtesy of Smith System Manufacturing Co.)

visual materials, and from manufacturers of office and school furniture. They
have been grouped here to show their multipurpose and specific capabilities.

Standard Shelving:

   8 mm films

   Kits, realia, or any material in a container which will fit on adjustable
   shelving.

   Phonorecords, 7″ and 10″

   Tape recordings

Files:

   Vertical files, for unframed mounted or unmounted pictures, pamphlets,
   folded charts and maps, transparencies, and guides, come in three sizes:
   Correspondence or letter file: for 9″x12″ mounts.
   Legal file: for 10″x15″ mounts. This is the most commonly recommended size.
   X-Ray or jumbo file: for 15″x18″ mounts, also accommodates recordings and
   overhead transparencies.

   Horizontal file drawers for larger unframed mounted, unmounted, and in
   portfolio prints, posters, charts and maps. A recommended size is 32″ front-to-
   back by 43″ wide by 2″ deep. They are available in 5-drawer units, with
   fabric dust covers for each drawer. A very convenient counter height cabinet
   can be made from two units (10 drawers).

Cabinets, both mobile and stationary:

> Framed art prints. These are usually designed with a series of slots wide enough to store pictures in an upright position without damaging the frames.

> Unframed mounted prints and disc recordings.

> Correlated materials: filmstrips, records, and guides.

> Filmstrips. Shallow drawers are compartmentalized by wires or partitions for single filmstrips.

> Multi-media: filmstrips, filmstrip cartridges, records, tapes, 8mm reels and cartridges, slides, transparencies.

> Microforms.

> Motion pictures, 16mm, equipped with racks.

> Records and tapes.

> Rolled-up charts, maps, prints. These are composed of a series of pigeon-holes of various sizes and depths.

> Slides and transparencies, with a light panel for viewing.

Racks:

> Horizontal or vertical storage of 16mm film cans.

> Phonograph records; small prints.

> Large framed and unframed prints.

> Hanging maps and charts, and vertical file materials. These may be mounted on the wall, the ceiling, on cabinets or on the side panels of shelves.

Modular Units:

> Shelving which may be lengthened, shortened, or re-arranged by adding or subtracting units. They may also be adjusted to permit the placement of film racks, shelf filmstrip holders, cartridge filmstrip trays, audio tape containers, filing boxes or bins for phonograph records, prints and transparencies.

> Cabinets with interchangeable modular height drawers for filmstrips, 8mm cartridges, and audio tapes.

Special Purpose Units:

> Filmstrips: Holders designed for placement on book shelves; easel boxes; wall hung container panels.

> Records: Browsing bins.

> Slides: Pockets in sheet form or in panels.

Sources for Mounting Equipment and Materials:

> Brandywine Photo Chemical Co., Avondale, Pa. 19311. Manufacturers *Spray-Mount* photo adhesive.

Eastman Kodak Co., 343 State St., Rochester, N.Y. 14650. Manufactures dry-mount tissue.

Krylon, 18 W. Airy St., Norristown, Pa. 19401. Manufactures plastic spray.

Seal, Inc., Brook St., Shelton, Conn. 06484. Manufactures dry-mount presses, tissue, and laminating film.

Additional information can be obtained from the following sources:

Kemp, Jerrold E. *Planning and Producing Audiovisual Materials.* 1st rev. ed. San Francisco: Chandler, 1968.

Weber, Olga, ed. *Audiovisual Market Place.* New York: Bowker, 1969.

Wittich, Arno, and Charles F. Schuller. *Audiovisual Materials: Their Nature and Use.* 4th ed. New York: Harper & Row, 1967.

PART II
THE PRACTICE

8

EXAMPLES AND
PRACTICAL PROCEDURES

Part 2 demonstrates the practical application of general procedures to specific types of material. It is structured to illustrate the actual work flow and routines involved in preparing each kind of audiovisual resource for patron use. Where previous discussion has adequately covered selection, acquisition, equipment, and storage facilities, these topics are not repeated. However, if the peculiarities of a certain material warrant additional comment, further analysis of these subjects is included. This more detailed information is meant to supplement and be used with that already presented. Wherever sources are given they are listed only as a sampling of those available and do not represent endorsement of one product in preference to others. To share ideas which experience has proven successful, recommended practices and helpful hints are suggested. The cataloging and physical processing of each type of material is fully treated. This demonstration approach provides a ready reference tool to answer the ever-recurring question: "How should this particular material be handled?"

A note. Cards in this section which are marked with an asterisk(*) are samples only and *do not* represent real items.

ART PRINTS
SYMBOL: PA   COLOR CODE: SALMON

Due to constant advancement in technical processes, the quality of art prints continues to improve. Because newer methods of reproduction and increased demand have lowered costs, an art print collection is now feasible for almost all libraries. Obtainable in a variety of formats—mounted, unmounted, framed, and in portfolio—art prints can be used both by the individual and the group. Previously limited to larger institutions, they are now an important resource in school, public, academic, and special libraries because of their manifold values in education, creativity, acculturation, aesthetic appreciation, and research.

More and more libraries are now acquiring collections of original prints. These are impressions made from a plate fashioned by the artist himself, and signed by him. Some of the various methods of acquisition are outright purchase, purchase on a commission basis, rental, and loan.

SELECTION CRITERIA

Look for these additional specific points of quality:

Authenticity of reproduction of the original art work with regard to detail, color, depth dimension, and size proportions.
Aesthetic mounting and framing.
Suitability of overall size for intended use, storage, and circulation.
Durability of color, stock, mounts, and frames.

SOME SELECTION SOURCES

Bartran, Margaret. *Guide to Color Reproductions.* New York: Scarecrow Press, 1966.

Bettmann, Otto, ed. *Bettmann Portable Archive.* New York: Picture House, 1966.

Clapp, Jane. *Art Reproductions.* New York: Scarecrow Press, 1961.

New York Graphic Society. *Fine Art Reproductions: Old and Modern Masters.* 8th ed. Greenwich, Conn.: New York Graphic Society, 1968.

UNESCO. *Catalogue of Colour Reproductions of Paintings Prior to 1860.* 7th ed. New York: Columbia Univ. Press, 1964. Frequent editions.

————. *Catalogue of Colour Reproductions of Paintings: 1860–1965.* 8th ed. New York: Columbia Univ. Press, 1966. Frequent editions.

The prints listed in these last two catalogs were selected by experts from many color reproductions submitted by publishers of all countries. The description of each print includes information about the process used in painting, the printer and publisher, the size, and the price.

CATALOGING

Art prints of sufficient value to be considered relatively permanent acquisitions should be cataloged. Those miscellaneous unmounted prints of various sizes which are of ephemeral worth because of their mediocrity of reproduction, material, and sustained subject interest (e.g., clipped from magazines) should be treated as Vertical File Material.

COLLATION   Number of mounted or unmounted prints if more than 1, dimensions, color statement, special format (e.g., wood frame; in portfolio).

NOTES   Type of art, media of original.

OPTIONAL   Date of execution, location of original.

PA
42

Muscular dynamism, or, Unique forms of continuity in space, by Umberto Boccioni. Art
print. London, Gimpel Fils.
21"x26", color, mounted with plastic frame.

Reproduction of a sculpture in polished
bronze, 1913, 43½" high. Original in the Mu-
seum of Modern Art, Milan. Study of a figure
in motion.

FUTURISM (ART)/ SCULPTURE/ Boccioni, Umberto/
t: Unique forms of continuity in space.

*Single mounted print.
Accession classification system.
Title main entry.

PA
759.4
Da

Dancers and ballet scenes, by Edgar Degas. Art
print. New York, Penn Prints, n.d.
8 unmounted prints, 11"x14", color, in portfolio.

Original paintings in the Louvre, Paris.
Ballerina on stage; Ballet study; Before the
ballet; Dancer with bouquet; Dancing class; Re-
hearsal; Taking the bow; Two dancers on the
stage.

BALLET/ PAINTINGS, FRENCH/ Degas, Hilaire
Germain Edgar/ t

Set of unmounted prints.
Dewey Decimal classification system.
Title main entry.
Optional: Added entries or analytics for individual paintings. The tracing "t"
designates an added entry for each title in the contents note.

PA
759.4   Degas' Dancers and ballet scenes. Art print.
De   New York, Penn Prints, n.d.
               8 unmounted prints, 11"x14", color, in port-
           folio.

               Original paintings in the Louvre, Paris.
               Ballerina on stage; Ballet study; Before the
           ballet; Dancer with bouquet; Dancing class; Re-
           hearsal; Taking the bow; Two dancers on the
           stage.

           BALLET/ PAINTINGS, FRENCH/ Degas, Hilaire
           Germain Edgar/ t: Dancers and ballet scenes.
           t

Set of unmounted prints.
Dewey Decimal classification system.
Filing title main entry, using possessive form of artist's name as first word of title.

PA
759.4   Degas, Hilaire Germain Edgar
De   Dancers and ballet scenes. Art print.   New
           York, Penn Prints, n.d.
               8 unmounted prints, 11"x14", color, in port-
           folio.

               Original paintings in the Louvre, Paris.
               Ballerina on stage; Ballet study; Before the
           ballet; Dancer with bouquet; Dancing class; Re-
           hearsal; Taking the bow; Two dancers on the
           stage.
           BALLET/ PAINTINGS, FRENCH/ t

Set of unmounted prints.
Dewey Decimal classification system.
Artist main entry.
Optional: Added entries or analytics for each title in contents note.

PA
759.4
Da
        Dancers and ballet scenes.
    Penn Prints.
        8 Prints.

PA
42

    Muscular dynamism. Gimpel Fils.

Circulation Card: Include number of items if more than one.

Pocket for mounted prints may be pasted on back; or circulation card may be
    kept at desk.

PHYSICAL PROCESSING

    Art prints are processed in the same manner as charts and pictures. Whenever
possible, mounted prints should be purchased. Generally, they are less expensive
than the staff time, the initial equipment cost, and the supplies required for the
mounting process. It is also wise to try to obtain prints whose overall dimensions
are of a standard size which will fit into readily available files or drawers.

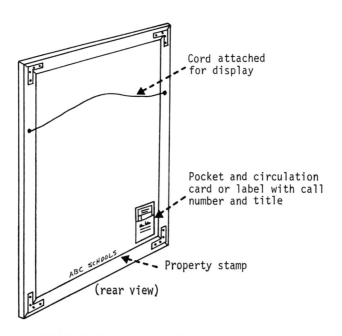

Cord attached
for display

Pocket and circulation
card or label with call
number and title

Property stamp

ABC SCHOOLS

(rear view)

FIGURE 20. LABELING PROCEDURE FOR FRAMED PRINT

    Whether to procure framed or unframed pictures is a decision which will
vary with local conditions and with particular prints. In many instances the cost
of a frame may exceed that of the print itself. Some prints may require a more
expensive frame than do others, and some libraries may have access to less expensive local framing services.
    For hanging purposes, if prints are purchased mounted with wood frames,
attach eye hooks to the back of the frame about one-third of the way down from
the top and thread with picture-hanging wire.
    If desired, a pocket for the circulation card, and explanatory notes about the
work of art may be pasted on the reverse of print.
    Label back of picture and carrying case if one is provided.

BIBLIOGRAPHY

Cain, Robert E. "The Original Print." *Library Journal* 91, No. 19 (Nov. 1, 1966): 5323–26.

Foster, Donald L. "A Picasso in Every Library," *Wilson Library Bulletin* 37 (Sept. 1962): 58–60.

Teller, Oscar. "Picasso in the Nursery." *School Library Journal* 11, No. 4 (Dec. 1964): 36–38.

See also Bibliography under Pictures.

CHARTS
SYMBOL: PC   COLOR CODE: SALMON

DEFINITION   A sheet which, in list, picture, table, or diagram form, provides information quickly and simply; a visual summary of processes or relationships.

CATALOGING

COLLATION   Number of mounted or unmounted charts if more than 1, dimensions, color statement, special format.

```
PC
500      Elementary science charts, by Milton O. Pella.
El            Chart.   Nystrom, 1960.
              160 charts, 18½"x24", color, mounted on a
         metal easel.
              Teaching guide.

              Living things.-Machines.- Magnets.- Electri-
         city.- Heat.- Matter.- Air and fire.- Light.-
         Sound.- Seasons and climate.- Geographic terms.-
         Rocks and minerals.- Conservation.- Universe and
         space.

         SCIENCE
```

Set of mounted charts.

Dewey Decimal classification system.

Optional: Contents note showing broad subject grouping. Added entry for author of charts.

PC
1321   Plant function and structure. Chart.   Denoyer-
                Geppert.
                4 charts, 40"x28", color, mounted on muslin,
            spring roller.

                Toadstools.- Pore bearing and prickly fungi.-
            Disk and coral fungi.- Coral, glovose and truf-
            fle fungi.

            FUNGI/ PLANTS

Set of mounted charts.

Accession classification system.

Optional: Contents note. Notation "n.d." for date not known.

PHYSICAL PROCESSING

FOLDED CHARTS   File in a regular file cabinet. Label on reverse of chart so that when it is folded for filing its label shows in upper corner. Keep circulation card in file at charge-out desk.

UNMOUNTED, UNFOLDED CHARTS   If stored in special hanging racks, in thin drawers, or on spring rollers, label front or back of chart or visible end of roller.

   If rolled up separately in mailing tubes, label chart and outside of container.

MOUNTED CHARTS   Mount charts on suitably stiff and heavy material such as Chipboard No. 4, available in gray only.

   Adherents for mounting:

   Rubber cement applied to both chart and mount is allowed to become tacky before chart is placed in position on mount.
   Dry mounting is done with a special dry mount tissue and an iron, or with a dry mount press.
   Wet mounting on muslin is not recommended unless skilled personnel and good facilities are available.

   To facilitate hanging and displaying, make pin or grommeted holes in upper corners of mount or attach Dennison suspension eyelets.
   Label on outside edge, at top or bottom, whichever is most visible.

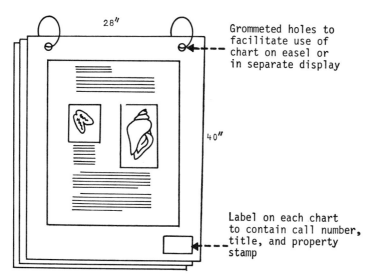

28"

Grommeted holes to
facilitate use of
chart on easel or
in separate display

40"

Label on each chart
to contain call number,
title, and property
stamp

FIGURE 21. MOUNTED CHARTS

BIBLIOGRAPHY

See Bibliography under "Pictures."

DIORAMAS
SYMBOL: DD   COLOR CODE: BROWN STRIP

DEFINITION   A three-dimensional miniature scene made with figures, objects, and background, to create an illusion of reality.

CATALOGING

COLLATION   Dimensions (width x height x depth), color statement, format.
ACCOMPANYING MATERIALS   Descriptive statement of any additional pieces provided.

RA
582
F1

      Flowers of California. Diorama.   Jefferson,
        Calif., Columbus Elementary School, 1966.
        12"x10"x5", color, Masonite box with hinged
lid. 4-6.
        25 additional stand-up illustrations of wild
flowers and background scenery, with plywood
stands.

        Scenes and flowers may be rearranged to show
growth locales. Background is a map of California on which flowers are shown geographical-
ly.

CALIFORNIA/ WILD FLOWERS

---

*Diorama.
Dewey Decimal classification system.
Locally produced material.

RA
2040

      Favorite stories then and now. Diorama.
        Scenes from Andersen's Fairy tales. Kensing-
        ton, Ohio, Washington Elementary School, 1965.
        36"x36"x12", color, cardboard with clear
plastic cover.

        Produced by fourth grade students. Four
scenes, each illustrating a different tale: The
red shoes; The ugly duckling; The Snow Queen;
The little match girl.

FAIRY TALES/ Andersen, Hans Christian

---

*Diorama.
Accession classification system.
Locally produced material.
Optional: Title analytics for each of the four tales illustrated, designated by the
    tracing "t."

```
        The ugly duckling.  In
RA
2040    Favorite stories then and now.  Diorama.  Scenes
        from Andersen's Fairy tales.  Kensington,
        Ohio, Washington Elementary School, 1965.
```

*Diorama.
  Title analytic.

PHYSICAL PROCESSING

Label outside of box.
On the inside of the lid or box, paste an inventory of any additional figures included, identifying each item.
A large plastic bag may be used for a protective covering if necessary.

EQUIPMENT
SYMBOL: EQ   COLOR CODE: GRAY STRIP

DEFINITION   Those machines and devices essential for reproduction and presentation of audiovisual materials. Apparatus and supplies necessary for maintenance are not considered.
Without adequate equipment nonbook materials are of little value. An in-depth treatment of the selection and operation of audiovisual equipment goes beyond the scope of this work and merits a volume of its own. Such detailed information will be found in:

Erickson, Carlton W. H. *Administering Instructional Media Programs*. New York: Macmillan, 1968. 660 pp.

Brown, James W., and Richard B. Lewis. *A-V Instruction: Media and Methods.* 3rd ed. New York: McGraw-Hill, 1969.

The type and amount of equipment available for the utilization of the materials determine how well the library meets the patron's need. The nonbook materials selected for the modern library are intended primarily for the use of the individual. The equipment provided, therefore, must have the capability for individualized use. Thus, for visuals, rear projection equipment (see Figure 9, p. 23), should be acquired so that they can be viewed in the library under normal lighting. By furnishing separate record and tape players or a sophisticated dial retrieval system, individualized listening service is given.

Each library has its own particular needs that must be met by the equipment collection. To ensure that such equipment adequately accomplishes this task the library should clearly state the specifications or characteristics which are essential for the kind of service required from it. In selecting equipment, the lowest price should not be the paramount criterion. Since equipment will receive very hard use the higher priced quality equipment may often really be the more economical. Requiring less maintenance and consequent down time, it will give the individual patron more dependable service. When the library has determined the most suitable equipment by type and brand, it is important that it be recommended as standard.

There are several definite advantages to standardization. It is easier to train personnel and instruct patrons in the operation of the equipment. Familiarity obtained by working on standardized brands or types facilitates maintenance. And, economies are gained in quantity purchases of equipment and in stocking spare parts and bulbs.

To assure continuous availability, back-up equipment is needed to replace a machine that has broken down. To keep down time to a minimum a maintenance program is essential, not only to make repairs quickly, but also to carry out preventative measures. A plan for replacement of equipment on a regular basis should also be in force. Since changes are so rapid in audiovisual equipment, budget planning should include funds to add new equipment to meet library needs.

CATALOGING

Two cards only are necessary for equipment: a reference card for the public catalog and a shelf-list card.

MAIN ENTRY   Enter under a standard description of type of machine, e.g., motion picture projector—16mm slide projector, disregarding brand name.

CALL NUMBER   The capital letter symbol designating the type of material that the equipment reproduces is placed below the symbol EQ. For example, the call number of a filmstrip projector is EQ of a record player, EQ of an 8mm motion
FS;   RD;
picture projector, EQ
ML.

CLASSIFICATION NUMBER   Since no subject classification applies, an accession number is assigned to each piece of equipment.

REFERENCE CARD FOR THE PUBLIC CATALOG

The purpose of this card is to inform the user that audiovisual equipment is available. One card for each type of equipment is therefore sufficient, e.g., tape recorder, overhead projector. It is unnecessary to provide a separate card giving specific information for each piece of equipment. Since the card refers to a group of holdings no accession number will appear as part of the call number.

NOTES   Location of the equipment and/or where to request it, e.g., located in audiovisual storage room.

```
EQ
SL          Slide projector.  Equipment.

            Request at Circulation Desk.
```

Equipment.
Reference card for the public catalog.
No accession or Dewey number.

SHELF-LIST CARD

The information entered on the shelf-list card for each piece of equipment includes: accession number; brand name; model; serial number; source of purchase; date of purchase; price; accompanying material or accessories.
A composite shelf-list card listing each piece of equipment may be made, or a separate card for each machine may be provided.

OPTIONAL   Description of special features, e.g., semi-automatic, remote push-button control, maintenance, supplies, and service record.

```
EQ
SL              Slide projector.  Equipment.

7               Airequipt Festival 250 #26802, Mf 1/64 99.95
24 ·            Airequipt Autostack 550 #8342, Mf 9/65 109.95;
                    slide file 3.98; slide handler 1.98
101             Eastman Carousel 800 #14360, PH 6/66 144.50;
                    slide tray 2.95
295             Realist 400 Automatic #8327, PH 12/67 29.95; 6
                    slide trays 5.95
```

Equipment.
Composite shelf-list card.
Call number does not include accession number.
Continuation cards made as needed for additional acquisitions.

```
EQ
SL              Slide projector.  Equipment.  Eastman Carousel
101                 800 #14360, PH 6/66 144.50; slide tray 2.95.

                    2x2 slides, automatic, pushbutton remote con-
                trol.

1/67   New lamp DEK 500 watt
```

Equipment.
Separate shelf-list card for each machine.
Accession number is part of call number.
Optional: Descriptive notes, service record.

```
EQ
SL
101  Slide projector.  Eastman
       Carousel 800 #14360
       w/instructions, slide tray
```


Circulation card.

Call number includes accession number.

List all accompanying material and/or accessories, which will have the same call number as the equipment.

If the library does not wish to make a circulation card for each piece of equipment it may devise a sign-out sheet which provides spaces to enter the same pertinent information as is shown on the circulation card.

PHYSICAL PROCESSING

Label equipment, accompanying material, accessories, carrying case, with ownership and call number (accession number included).

OPERATING INSTRUCTIONS   If these are not already provided they should be pasted on the equipment or case in an easily visible location.

Provide inventory of accompanying material and/or accessories, pasted in the most suitable position.

BIBLIOGRAPHY

Various sources are available for information on equipment, including the following regular periodical features: "Buyer's Guide" in each first-of-the-month issue of *Library Journal;* "Equipment" in *School Library Journal,* which supplements the *LJ* column, and is geared especially for instructional programs in school libraries; "Equipment in Review" in *Audiovisual Instruction.* Also, various supplements to *Educational Product Report* will be helpful, in addition to the following large-scale sources:

Eboch, Sidney C. *Operating Audio-Visual Equipment.* rev ed. San Francisco: Chandler, 1968.

National Audio-Visual Association (NAVA). *Audio-Visual Equipment Directory.* Fairfax, Va.: NAVA, annual.

Pula, Fred J. *Application and Operation of Audiovisual Equipment in Education.* New York: Wiley, 1968.

School Product News. Industrial Publishing Co., 614 Superior Ave. West, Cleveland, Ohio 44113. A free, monthly magazine.

FILMSTRIPS
SYMBOL: FS   COLOR CODE: GREEN

DEFINITION   A strip of film (usually 35mm) that presents a sequence of related still pictures for projection. In the case of silent filmstrips, printed captions often appear beneath each picture or frame to assist in communicating ideas.

A variety of *sound* filmstrips are also available. The disc or tape recording which accompanies the filmstrip is usually synchronized with it by an audible or inaudible cue signalling an advance to the next frame. As new equipment is created sound filmstrips are being produced as one unit. Some of these are the tape-cartridge filmstrip, which houses both the filmstrip and the tape in a cartridge that drops into position in the projector; and the Soundstrip (Kalart), which photographically records sound on the same film that carries the pictures, permitting storage of the entire program in a small can.

The suitability of the filmstrip as a resource for the individual demands special emphasis. Equipment for viewing is simple to operate and each person is free to control his own pace. A wide subject variety is available, and according to the specific needs of the individual, a single filmstrip may often be used as a multi-subject resource. In addition, the relatively low cost of filmstrips and facilities and equipment for their viewing, contribute to the feasibility of their inclusion in all library collections.

EQUIPMENT

Many different types and sizes of filmstrip projectors for individual, and small and large group viewing are now on the market. They may be manually or automatically operated, and some combine in one machine the capability to reproduce filmstrips, slides, recordings or tapes. If filmstrips in cassettes are acquired compatible equipment is also required. Development in the design of filmstrip projectors should be closely followed since many of the new features permit greater ease of operation. Projectors such as the cassette sound (DuKane) and the automatic can-to-can rewind (Graflex) illustrate this trend.

FIGURE 22. CASSETTE SOUND FILMSTRIP PROJECTOR FOR LIBRARY USE. *Such rear projection equipment permits the use of filmstrips in normally lighted rooms, avoiding the necessity for special rooms for film projection.* (Photograph courtesy of DuKane Corp.)

CATALOGING

The cataloging of a single filmstrip is simple and straightforward. However, problems are generated with the inclusion of other materials such as records, tapes, manuals and scripts, which are essential to the understanding of the filmstrip. Further complications result from the variety of different ways in which producers provide and package these materials. A single manual may refer to six filmstrips in a series, with only one manual supplied, or a separate manual may appear for each filmstrip. With sound filmstrips, the present practice of recording a different filmstrip on either side of the record limits the use of the two filmstrips to one user, unless a duplicate record is available. With so many variations of this type existing, it is evidently impossible to formulate specific rules to cover the cataloging of every deviation. Methods of treating some of the more commonly occurring combinations of materials are discussed in the chapter on cataloging. In all instances the cataloger's decision on how to handle these resources should be based on the general rule that the cataloging should facilitate the use of the material by the individual, and for as many individuals as possible. Thus, according to the peculiarities of each particular package, the material may be cataloged as several separate items, as a series, as one kit, or split up as several kits. The cataloging examples illustrate several different methods of treatment.

COLLATION   Number of frames, color statement, width in millimeters. Since the standard width is 35 mm, the width may be omitted unless it is other than standard. Any different format necessitating special equipment should be noted, e.g., cassette.

```
FS
2143        Christmas customs.  Filmstrip.  Filmfax, 1952.
               36 fr., color, 35mm.

               Portrays the origin of many of our Christmas
            customs, including Santa Claus and Christmas
            trees.  With captions.



            CHRISTMAS
```

Single filmstrip, silent.
Accession classification system.
Optional: added entry for producer.

```
FS
92      James Russell Lowell.  Filmstrip.   EBE, 1954.
Lo         47 fr., color.  American poets.

           Depicts the life of Lowell, his success as
        a poet, lawyer, humorist, journalist, educator
        and politician.  Includes excerpts from his
        poems.  Captioned drawings.


        LOWELL, JAMES RUSSELL/ POETS/ ser
```

Single filmstrip, silent.
Dewey Decimal classification system.
Individual biography: initial letters of biographee's surname below class number
    replace those of title main entry.
Filmstrips in a series, with accompanying material: 9 filmstrips, 1 recording syn-
    chronized with 5 of the filmstrips, 1 guide. See also example under Kits.

```
FS
811     Riddles.  Filmstrip.  Eye Gate, 1964.
Ri         40 fr., color.  Enjoying poetry.   4-8.
        Teachers manual.

           Presents several short riddles in verse to
        encourage discussion of the imagery of words.
        Includes I met a man with three eyes, by John
        Ciardi.


        FIGURES OF SPEECH/ POETRY/ ser
```

Filmstrip no. 1 of a series cataloged individually.
Dewey Decimal classification system.
Accompanying material: call number & title the same as those of filmstrip, are not
    repeated.

```
FS
811     Riddles.      Eye Gate.
Ri
              (Guide)
```

Circulation card for a filmstrip with accompanying material stored separately.
Parentheses indicate accompanying material available but not included on check-
    out card.

```
FS
811     Riddles.      Eye Gate.
Ri
     Guide.
```

Circulation card for accompanying material stored separately.
Identify kind of material.

```
FS
811        Limericks.  Filmstrip.  Eye Gate, 1964.
Li             42 fr., color.  Enjoying poetry.  4-8.
           Teachers manual: Riddles FS 811 Ri.

           Explains how a limerick is constructed and
       gives students an opportunity to complete some
       last lines.


       POETRY/ ser
```

Filmstrip no. 2 of a series cataloged individually.
Accompanying material: Call number and title different from those of filmstrip are
    noted.

```
FS
811      Limericks.  Eye Gate.
Li
             (Guide: Riddles FS 811 Ri)
```

Circulation card for a filmstrip with accompanying material of a different call
    number and title.

```
FS
811          Story poem.  Filmstrip.  Eye Gate, 1964.
St               5 fs., color.  Enjoying poetry.  4-8.
                 Teachers manual: Riddles FS 811 Ri; Record,
             disc: 2s, 12", 33.3 rpm.

                 Casey at the bat, by E.L. Thayer. 30fr.-
             Leak in the dike, by Phoebe Cary. 37fr.- Paul
             Revere's ride, by H.W. Longfellow. 30fr.-
             Daniel Boone, by Arthur Gutterman. 32fr.- Bar-
             bara Frietchie, by J.G. Whittier. 29fr.

             POETRY/ t/ ser
```

Filmstrips no. 5–9 of a series, synchronized with 1 record, cataloged as a set, sound.

Accompanying material: 1 with different call no. & title, 1 with same call no. & title. Both stored separately.

Title added entry for each filmstrip listed in contents.

```
FS
811       Story poem.      Eye Gate.
St            (Guide: Riddles FS 811 Ri;
          Record)
      5fs.
```

Circulation card for filmstrips cataloged as a set, with accompanying material stored separately.

```
FS
811      Story poem.      Eye Gate.
St
     Record, disc
```


Circulation card for accompanying material to filmstrips cataloged as a set, stored separately.

```
FS
811      Casey at the bat.      Eye Gate
St
              see
     Story poem.
```


Circulation cross reference card from title of an individual filmstrip cataloged as part of a set.

Enjoying poetry. Filmstrip. Eye Gate, 1964.

811 Ri	Riddles.
811 Li	Limericks.
811 Sh-1	Short poems, part 1.
811 Sh-2	Short poems, part 2.
811 St	Story poem: Casey at the bat; Leak in the dike; Paul Revere's ride; Daniel Boone; Barbara Frietchie.

Composite series card. Four filmstrips cataloged individually, five filmstrips cataloged as a set.

SOUND FILMSTRIPS   Two different filmstrips, each synchronized with a recording on either side of one disc, or on one tape.

TITLE MAIN ENTRY   The title of the filmstrip on side 1 of the recording is the title main entry. It is immediately followed by the title of the filmstrip recorded on side 2.

COLLATION   Number of filmstrips, number of frames in each filmstrip, color statement.

ACCOMPANYING MATERIAL—OPTIONAL   Notation of running time in minutes after physical description of the record.

Sound filmstrips in a series, consisting of 8 filmstrips recorded on 4 discs, and 1 guide. This may be treated as 4 separate units. A circulation cross reference card from the title of the filmstrip on side 2 of each record to the title main entry will speed up check-out procedure.

```
FS
398      The wise little hen.   Jiminy Cricket in Dutch.
Wi           Filmstrip.    EBF, 1959.
             2 fs., 66, 81 fr., color.  Walt Disney's
         Tales of Jiminy Cricket, series 2.   K-3.
             Teacher's guide; Record, disc: 2s, 12", 33.3
         rpm.

             Record synchronized with filmstrips.

         FABLES/ NETHERLANDS- FICTION/ t: Jiminy Cricket
         in Dutch./ ser
```

Filmstrip, sound. 2 filmstrips on 1 record.
Dewey Decimal classification system.
Filmstrips no. 1 and 2 of a series cataloged as a unit.

```
FS
Do       Donald's apple orchard.   The grasshopper and the
             ants.  Filmstrip.   EBF, 1959.
             2 fs., 82, 88 fr., color.  Walt Disney's
         Tales of Jiminy Cricket, series 2.   K-3.
             Teacher's guide: The wise little hen FS 398
         Wi; Record, disc: 2s, 12", 33.3 rpm.

             Record synchronized with filmstrips.

         FABLES/ ORCHARDS- FICTION/ t: The grasshopper
         and the ants./ ser
```

Filmstrip, sound. 2 filmstrips on 1 record.
Fiction.
Filmstrips no. 3 and 4 of a series cataloged as a unit.
Accompanying material: guide has the same title and call number as the first unit
     under which it was cataloged.

```
              Walt Disney's Tales of Jiminy Cricket, series 2.
                  Filmstrip.  EBF, 1959-60.
  398  Wi    The wise little hen.  Jiminy Cricket in Dutch.
       Do    Donald's apple orchard.  The grasshopper and the
                  ants.
  398  Co    The country cousin.  The golden touch.
       Le    Lend a paw.  Bootle Beetle.




       x Tales of Jiminy Cricket, series 2.
```

Composite series card for sound filmstrips.

```
  FS
  596       Animals with backbones.  Filmstrip.  EBE, 1964.
  An            7 fs., 60 fr. each, color.  Basic life
            science

            What is a vertebrate?- Discovering fishes.-
        Discovering amphibians.- Discovering birds.- Ob-
        serving birds in nature.- Discovering mammals.-
        Discovering reptiles.
            Basic concepts of life presented in the 5
        vertebrate classes shown in their natural
        habitats.

        AMPHIBIA/ BIRDS/ FISHES/ MAMMALS/ REPTILES/ VER-
        TEBRATES
```

Filmstrips cataloged as a set.

```
FS
596
An
        Animals with backbones.    EBE.

    7 fs.
```


Circulation card for filmstrips cataloged as a set.
Specify number of filmstrips.

PHYSICAL PROCESSING

SINGLE FILMSTRIPS   Label leader of filmstrip. Affix label with call number to lid of filmstrip can so that the original label showing title remains exposed. A three-line call number can be typed on a ½″x½″ label, pressure sensitive, available in rolls which can be fed into the typewriter. It is advisable to order these labels 6-up, 8-up, or in a sequence which will permit most of the call numbers of the individually cataloged filmstrips of an entire series to be typed straight across.

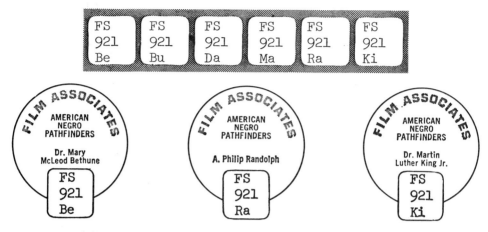

FORM 16. FILMSTRIP CANNISTER LABELS

Adhere label with ownership identification around the container. The C-Vue Call Label Protector provides an excellent permanent, and easily applied protection for this label. Pressure sensitive, made of a clear flexible plastic material, it measures 3"x1¼" and fits the height of the filmstrip can below the lid so that no trimming is necessary. It is available from Crossley-Van Deusen Co., Inc., Marcellus, N.Y., 13108.

FILMSTRIP SETS   Inside the lid of the box, or on the outside if the box does not have a lift-up lid, affix the inventory label showing number and title of each filmstrip in the set. Include the identifying inventory number on the label of each filmstrip.

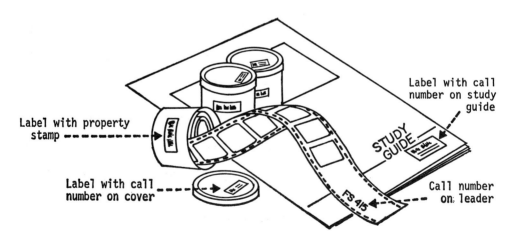

FIGURE 23. FILMSTRIPS AND STUDY GUIDE

FILMSTRIPS WITH RECORDS, TAPES, AND/OR GUIDES   Label records (see Recordings) and guides so that they may be identified with the filmstrip. If only one guide is provided for several different filmstrips, underline on it the title of the filmstrip under which it is cataloged. (See Figure 23.)

If possible, store filmstrip and its accompanying material together as a single unit in a fiber case (co-related container), properly labeled. If filmstrips, records, and manuals have to be stored separately, the label on each item should note the kind of accompanying material which completes the set, e.g., guide, record.

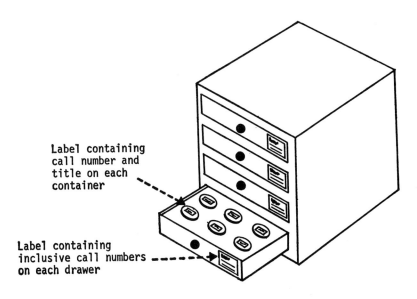

Label containing call number and title on each container

Label containing inclusive call numbers on each drawer

FIGURE 24. STORAGE FOR FILMSTRIPS

FILMSTRIPS: SHORTSTRIPS

DEFINITION A short filmstrip of fifteen frames or less, primarily intended for individual examination through a hand viewer. The strips may also be projected for group use. They are usually boxed in a set, with each strip treating a different specific subject related to the general subject of the set.

CATALOGING

COLLATION Number of shortstrips, number of frames in each strip, color statement, width in millimeters.

NOTES Contents note listing titles of individual shortstrips.

```
FS
500          Exploring with science.  Filmstrip.  EBE.
Ex              12 shortstrips, 14 fr. each, color, 35mm. K-3.
             Plastic hand-viewer.

             Old Mother Sun; Our planet earth; You and the
          universe; Seasons come and go; What day is it?
          When night comes; What is weather?; Power moves
          things; Meet the plant family; Meet the animal
          family; Meet the human family; You are alive.
             Drawings with easy-to-read short captions.

          SCIENCE
```

Set of shortstrips.
Dewey Decimal classification system.

PHYSICAL PROCESSING

Place an ownership and call number label on each shortstrip, on accompanying material, and on container. The circulation card may be laid in the box or inserted in a pocket pasted inside the lid. An inventory checklist of the shortstrip titles should also be pasted inside the lid if this does not appear elsewhere on the box.

FLASH CARDS
SYMBOL: PS   COLOR CODE: SALMON

DEFINITION Cards which may be manually held before the viewer for drill or recognition training of words, phrases, or symbols.

To make them easily adaptable to modern educational methods, flash cards are produced in a variety of combinations and packagings. Flash Charts, for example, incorporate programmed instruction. Provided with the cards (called charts) is a holder with view windows and a manipulative device that permit the individual to regulate his own pace in progressing through the material presented on each card.

CATALOGING

COLLATION Number of cards, dimensions, color statement, and notations on any special format.

```
PS
460       Teach me Spanish; the way to count, tell time,
Te            & talk about the weather.  Flash card.
          Parent Teacher Aids.
          51 flash cards, 3"x6", b&w.
          Instructions for use; Games to play; Key to
     Spanish pronunciation; English translations.

          Designed to provide elementary conversational
     experience.

     SPANISH LANGUAGE-STUDY AND TEACHING
```

Flash cards.
Dewey Decimal classification system.

PHYSICAL PROCESSING

Stamp ownership and write call number on the reverse side of each card, and on all accompanying material. All labelling should be done so as to avoid covering any of the text, should it appear on both sides of the card.

On the box, place the call number and ownership label so that it is easily visible when the material is on the shelf. If necessary, a title label should be added.

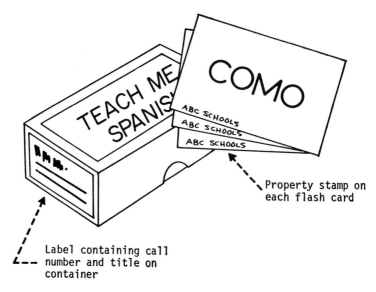

Property stamp on each flash card

Label containing call number and title on container

FIGURE 25. FLASH CARDS

ACQUISITION SOURCES

Follett Publishing Co., 1010 N. Washington Blvd., Chicago, Ill. 60607.
Garrard Publishing Co., 1607 N. Market St., Champaign, Ill. 61821.
Ideal School Supply Co., 11000 S. Lavergne Ave., Oaklawn, Ill. 60453.
Instructor Publications, Inc., Dansville, N.Y. 14437.
Milton Bradley Co., 74 Park St., Springfield, Mass. 01105.
World Research Co., 511 Stemmons Tower East, Dallas, Tex. 75207.

GAMES
SYMBOL: KL   COLOR CODE: BLACK STRIP

DEFINITION   A set of materials providing instruction and testing of skills while motivating the learner through play and competition.

CATALOGING

COLLATION   Numerical list of parts of the game, color statement, other pertinent information.

```
KL
45        Anagrams.  Game.   Milton Bradley.
             168 plastic tiles, green, in cardboard box.

          Designed to give practice in word and sen-
          tence building.




          VOCABULARY
```

Game.
Accession classification system.

```
KL
920       Meet the Presidents.  Game.   Milton Bradley.
 Me          34 metal presidential coins, folding map
          board of U.S., color, question and answer spin-
          ner.

          Historical facts about the Presidents, from
          Washington to Kennedy.  For 2, 3, or 4 players.


          PRESIDENTS- U.S./ U.S.- HISTORY
```

Game.
Dewey Decimal classification system.

PHYSICAL PROCESSING

Stamp ownership information on individual parts wherever possible, and on outside of box.

An inventory of parts and a pocket may be pasted inside the box cover. Place a call number label on the outside of the box in a visible position.

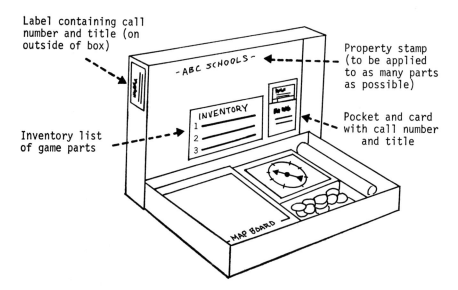

FIGURE 26. INSTRUCTIONAL GAMES

ACQUISITION SOURCES

Although new methods in education recognize the learning value of games, the number available for purchase is still limited. The following sources can supply helpful information about academic games.

Abt Associates, Inc., Cambridge, Mass. 02138.

Academic Games Associates, Center for Study of Social Organization of Schools, Johns Hopkins University, Baltimore, Md. 21218.

Board of Cooperative Educational Services, Center for Educational Services and Research, 845 Fox Meadow Rd., Yorktown Heights, N.Y. 10598.

CBS Learning Center, Social Studies Unit, 12 Station Rd., Princeton Junction, N.J. 08550.

Curriculum Development Center, Wellesley School System, Seawood Rd., Wellesley Hills, Mass. 02181.

Educational Development Center, 15 Mifflin Place, Cambridge, Mass. 02138.

Elementary Games Project, Industrial Relations Center, University of Chicago, 1225 E. 60th St., Chicago, Ill. 60637.

4-H Center Bookstore, 7100 Connecticut Ave., Washington, D.C. 20015.

High School Geography Project, University of Colorado, P.O. Box 1095, Boulder, Colo. 80302.

Holt, Rinehart & Winston, Inc., 383 Madison Ave., New York, N.Y. 10017.

Houghton Mifflin Co., Educational Division, 110 Trement St., Boston, Mass. 02107.

Information Services for Vocational Decisions, c/o Harvard Graduate School of Business, 220 Alewife Brook Parkway, Cambridge, Mass. 02138.

The Learning Center, Social Studies Dept., Princeton, N.J. 08540.

Charles E. Merrill, Inc., 1300 Alum Creek Dr., Columbus, Ohio 43216.

Milton Bradley Co., 74 Park St., Springfield, Mass. 01105.

Schoolhouse Visuals, Inc., 816 Thayer Ave., Silver Spring, Md. 20910.

Science Research Associates, Inc., 259 E. Erie St., Chicago, Ill. 60611.

Scott-Foresman & Co., 1900 E. Lake Rd., Glenview, Ill. 60025.

Western Behavioral Science Institute, 1121 Torre Pines Rd., La Jolla, Calif. 92037.

Wiff 'N Proof, P.O. Box 71, New Haven, Conn. 06501.

Yount, Dave, and Paul De Kock, El Capitan High School, Lakeside, Calif. 92040.

BIBLIOGRAPHY

"Academic Games." *School Library Journal* 15, No. 3 (Nov. 1968): 74.

Bock, Barbara. "Games as Teaching Tools." *Educate* 1, No. 2 (Sept. 1968): 26–31.

Boocock, Sarane S., and E. O. Schild, eds. *Simulation Games in Learning.* Beverly Hills: Sage Publications, 1968.

May, Lola J. "Educational Games in Math." *Audiovisual Instruction* 14, No. 2 (Feb. 1969): 27–29.

Shankman, Florence V. "Games Reinforce Reading Skills." *The Reading Teacher* 22, No. 3 (Dec. 1968): 262–64.

Simulation Games for the Social Studies Classroom. New York: Foreign Policy Association, 1968.

GLOBES
SYMBOL: DM   COLOR CODE: BROWN STRIP

TYPES OF GLOBES

Globes are available in a variety of sizes, mounts, and types. The most common diameter sizes are 8, 12, 16, 20, and 24 inches. Some of the different mounts include low and medium cradle mounts, with or without accessories such as latitude scales and horizon rings; and single or dual axes mounts which also may or may not have accessories attached. Globes may be permanently installed in the mount, or easily removable for closer individual study.

There are three principal types of globes: political globes, designed to show man-made features such as country and city boundaries; physical-political globes, which, while including political divisions, emphasize land and ocean formations; and slated-outline globes, which have a special surface made for easy marking and erasure. In addition, globe sections, transparent, and inflatable globes, and many special ones such as physical-relief, celestial, air-age, satellite, and moon globes, may be procured.

SELECTION CRITERIA

Look for these additional specific points of quality: accuracy in area sizes, shapes, directions, and distances; clarity of boundaries, special orientation lines, physical features and legends; non-glare, protective, transparent coating.

CATALOGING

IDENTIFICATION OF MATERIAL   If the globe is identified as such in the title, the designation "Globe" need not be repeated after the title.

IMPRINT   If the title names the person or corporate body responsible for the globe and it is the same as the producer or manufacturer, the name need not be repeated in the imprint. Include date, if known.

COLLATION   Diameter in inches; color statement; unusual surface or projection if it has not been stated in the title; special format, e.g., type of measure (meridian, horizon, time dial), mount.

ACCOMPANYING MATERIAL   Any guides and equipment which are to be used with the globe.

```
DM
912        Replogle comprehensive globe.
Re             16", color, political, non-illuminated, mov-
           able meridian, wood stand.
               See the world on a globe, by Mercedes Guyette,
           1951.

               Shows geographical relationships accurately.


           GLOBES
```

Globe.
Dewey Decimal classification system.
Optional: added entries for author and title of accompanying material.

PHYSICAL PROCESSING

Label or letter pedestal or hanger. Tie on any removable screws or parts. If a dust cover is used for protection, label it in the same manner as the pedestal.

KINESCOPES
SYMBOL: MP   COLOR CODE: BLUE

DEFINITION   A recording from a television source on 16mm sound motion picture film. It may be rebroadcast or projected as a standard 16mm sound film.

CATALOGING

COLLATION   Running time, sound, color statement, width in millimeters.

```
MP
792        Just imagine.  Motion picture (kinescope).
Ju            Indiana U. Audio-Visual Center, 1961.
              15 min., sd., b&w, 16mm.    4-9.

           A television program which shows how objects
           observed with imagination can spark creative ta-
           lent in children.  Students explain role they
           are to create and plan how all will participate.


           ACTING/ CREATION (LITERARY, ARTISTIC, ETC.)
```

Kinescope.
Dewey Decimal classification system.

PHYSICAL PROCESSING

Kinescopes are processed in the same manner as 16mm motion picture films.

SOME SOURCES OF INFORMATION

National Educational Television (NET) is one of the main sources for the rental or purchase of kinescopes. Information on programs may be obtained from the Audio-Visual Center, Indiana University (Bloomington, Ind. 47401), which publishes:

> *Catalog of Educational Films Produced and/or Distributed by the Indiana University Audio-Visual Center.* (NET film catalog). Frequent editions and supplements, 1964 to date.

> *Preview.* Periodical, issued irregularly, giving complete synopses and content notes of current releases.

KITS
SYMBOL: KT   COLOR CODE: BLACK STRIP

DEFINITION   A collection of two or more different types of materials giving information or instruction on one subject or related subjects.

CATALOGING

No collation is necessary since the contents note lists the items with any physical description needed.

```
KT
95              Iran introductory kit.  International Communica-
                   tions Foundation, 1962.
                4-12.

                Teacher's guide; 2 filmstrips: 61 fr., 68 fr.,
                color; 1 record, disc: 12", 33.3 rpm.; 16 pic-
                tures, 9¼"x12¼", color, with captions.
                A general survey of Iran.



                IRAN
```

Kit.
Accession classification system.
No material identification is needed since it is specified in the title.

```
KT
811          Enjoying poetry.  Kit.   Eye Gate, 1964.
En
                  Teacher's manual; 9 filmstrips, color; 1 re-
             cord, disc: 12", 33.3 rpm.
                  Presents riddles, limericks and story poems,
             explaining their construction and discussing the
             imagery of words.  Five filmstrips are synchro-
             nized with the recording.


             POETRY
```

Filmstrip set with record cataloged as a kit.
Dewey Decimal classification system.
Optional: Titles and number of frames of each filmstrip.
See also example under Filmstrips.

PHYSICAL PROCESSING

Label ownership and call number wherever possible on all items and on out-side of container.

Paste inventory of contents inside lid, and if necessary, a picture or diagram showing the placement of items in the container.

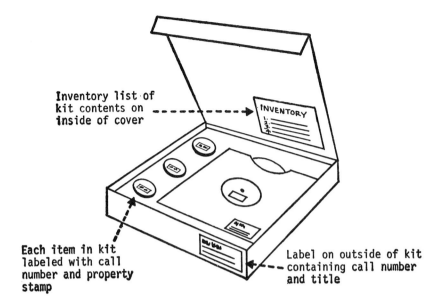

Inventory list of kit contents on inside of cover

INVENTORY

Each item in kit labeled with call number and property stamp

Label on outside of kit containing call number and title

FIGURE 27. RECORD AND FILMSTRIP KIT

MAPS
SYMBOL: PC   COLOR CODE: SALMON

TYPES OF MAPS

There are three basic types of maps, designated according to the primary features illustrated: physical maps, which picture terrain; political maps, which show governmental areas; special-purpose maps, which depict specific subjects such as population, vegetation, historical, economic, or literary development. Various combinations of these principal types, such as physical-political, are also available.

MAP PROJECTION

Projection is the method used to depict the three-dimensional spherical surface of the earth as a flat two-dimensional model. Different projections are employed to minimize the distortions which occur in area representation, in shapes, in distances, and in direction. Some of the most readily available projections among the variety now provided by map designers are: cylindrical, conical, azimuthal, Mercator, minimum-error, and equal-area.

SELECTION CRITERIA

Look for these additional specific points of quality: minimum distortion in areas, shapes, distance, direction; scale accuracy; recent revision showing current political changes; dominance of a significant geographical concept; symbols and legends at user's level; adequate locator devices.

CATALOGING

COLLATION   Number of maps if more than one, two sides (2s.) if material covers more than one side, dimensions, color statement, special format, and scale as given on the map.

ANNOTATION   Include notes on the type of map, and type of projection.

```
PC
4037        Middle America.  Map.    Rand, 1966.
               65"x45", color, spring roller, scale: 62mi:1".

               A simplified merged relief wall map, Sinusoi-
            dal Equal Area projection.  Includes all Central
            American countries, the Caribbean, and the West
            Indies.



            CENTRAL AMERICA/ MAPS
```

Single map.
Accession classification system.

```
PC
912        Rand McNally desk reference maps.
Ra             11 unmounted maps, 11"x15", color, scale
           varies.

               Merged relief maps of North America, South
           America, Europe, Asia, Africa, Australia, U.S.,
           Canada, Middle America, World; political map of
           the fifty United States.


           MAPS
```

Set of maps.
Dewey Decimal classification system.

PHYSICAL PROCESSING

See instructions for processing of "Charts" and "Pictures."

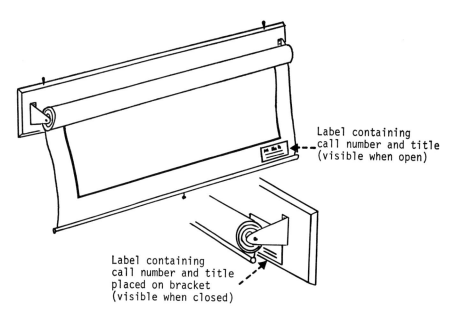

Label containing
call number and title
(visible when open)

Label containing
call number and title
placed on bracket
(visible when closed)

FIGURE 28. MAPS

BIBLIOGRAPHY

Brown, Lloyd A. "The Problem of Maps," *Library Trends* 13 (Oct. 1964): 215–25.

Marantz, Sylvia. "Maps in the Library," *School Libraries* 16, No. 2 (Winter, 1967): 25–28.

MICROFORMS

DEFINITION Reproductions in miniature, on transparent or opaque stock, of printed materials. Reduction varies, but is usually about 1/20 of the original. The various forms available include microfilm and microfiche, both transparent, and microcard and microprint, both opaque.

Machines for enlarging are required for viewing, and equipment and material must be compatible. Recently there has been a rapid multiplication in the kinds and shapes of microforms. As yet there is no standardization to restrict their variety or demand a system of machines so interrelated that their output can be converted automatically and inexpensively from one form to another. Various manufacturers provide readers in a wide span of performance sophistication, portability, and price. Those for large institutional use range from several hundred to well over a thousand dollars. Those for individual personal use may cost from under twenty dollars up to one hundred dollars.

SOURCES OF INFORMATION

Sources of information for materials and equipment are well presented by Albert Diaz in his article "Microreproduction Information Sources" (*Library Resources & Technical Services* 11, No. 2 (Spring 1967): 211–214). The librarian should keep abreast of current developments in the field through manufacturers' advertisements and brochures, *Library Technology Reports*, and articles in professional journals.

CATALOGING

Microfilms, microfiches, microcards and microprints are cataloged the same as the original work they reproduce. The symbol which identifies the kind of copy (FM, FF, PM) becomes part of the call number. A statement of the type (microfilm, microcard) is added, either two spaces after the title, or as a note.

MICROFILM
(TRANSPARENT)
SYMBOL: FM   COLOR CODE: GREEN

DEFINITION A roll of film, usually 35mm and in 100 foot reels, each frame presenting in proper order a partial or entire page of the original text. Microfilm in cartridges, and 16mm microfilm, are rapidly becoming more available. These require new, special equipment, or an adaptor that converts existing equipment to cartridge capability.

Specially designed metal filing cabinets are available for storing microfilms packaged in metal cans, cardboard boxes, or cartridges.

MICROFICHES
(TRANSPARENT)
SYMBOL: FF   COLOR CODE: GREEN

DEFINITION The frames of a microfilm in sheet form; or, a sheet of film on which, through further reduction of the original printing, many pages may be stored. Variations in format are aperture cards and jacketed film cards.

Since the customary sizes of microfiches are 3"x5" and 4"x6", they may be put in envelopes and filed in card file drawers.

The National Microfilm Association has reprinted for separate distribution a seventeen-page review of microfiche equipment which first appeared in the *NMA Journal*. This excellent survey of microfiche readers and reader-printers currently manufactured in the United States may be obtained from: Executive Secretary, National Microfilm Association (250 Prince George Street, P.O. Box 386, Annapolis, Md. 21404). Fifty cents (stamps accepted) should accompany order.

CATALOGING

COLLATION Below the note identifying the type of copy the number of reels is stated for microfilms, the number of sheets of film for microfiches.

OPTIONAL–NOTES Location of original if it is an out-of-print or rare work. Producer of copy.

```
FM
020.5      Library Journal.    Bowker.
Li             Bi-monthly
               Library has
           v.1-74, 1876-1949

               Microfilm copy of periodicals, made by Uni-
           versity Microfilms.
               74 reels.


           LIBRARY SCIENCE
```

Microfilms of a periodical.

MICROCARDS (OPAQUE)
SYMBOL: PM   COLOR CODE: SALMON

DEFINITION   A sensitized card, usually 3″x5″, containing several pages of a printed publication photographically reproduced from 16mm microfilm by contact printing.
Cards may be filed in standard library card catalog drawers.

MICROPRINTS (OPAQUE)
SYMBOL: PM   COLOR CODE: SALMON

DEFINITION   A 6″x9″ card on which numerous pages of a work are reproduced from 16mm microfilm by a form of offset printing.
Boxed in large sets, they may be shelved like books.

CATALOGING

COLLATION   Number of cards, or prints.

```
PM
943        Shirer, William L
Sh             The rise and fall of the Third Reich; a his-
           tory of Nazi Germany.    Simon, 1960.
                1245 p.

                Microcard copy of original book.
                15 cards.



           GERMANY- HISTORY- 1918-1945/ HITLER, ADOLF/ t
```

Microcards of a book.

PHYSICAL PROCESSING

For *all* types of microforms, place an ownership and call number label on the separate items and on the container.

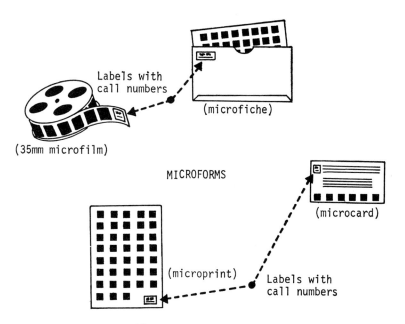

FIGURE 29. MICROFORMS

MOCK-UPS AND MODELS
SYMBOL: DM   COLOR CODE: BROWN STRIP

MOCK-UP   An operable imitation of a real device or process whose essential elements may be re-arranged, condensed, or enlarged for specific training or analysis by the learner.

MODEL   A three-dimensional representation of a real thing, made in exact size or on a smaller or larger scale. It may or may not be operational, an exact, or a simplified reproduction of the original.

CATALOGING

COLLATION   If the contents or descriptive notes include the physical description, no collation is necessary. If not, the collation states dimensions or size description, color statement, special format or mounting.

OPTIONAL   Manufacturer's catalog number following title. Since models often have similar titles, inclusion of the catalog number will avoid confusion.

```
DM
63           Eye - anatomy of sight, no. S220.  Mock-up.
                Ideal.

                 Twice life-size eyeball made to move real-
             istically in eye socket.




             EYE
```

Mock-up.
Accession classification system.

```
DM
611        Human torso and head, no. AM-98.  Model.    Nys-
Hu             trom.
               Teacher's guide: Functional health training;
           Code key.

               Simplified life-size model with eight remov-
           able parts, painted and coded, made of plastic.
           For students of beginning anatomy.


           ANATOMY
```

Model.
Dewey Decimal classification system.

PHYSICAL PROCESSING

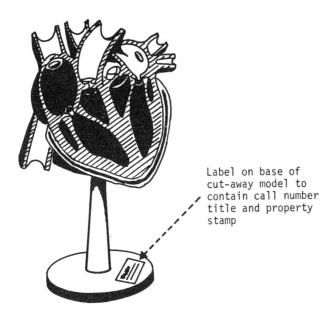

Label on base of
cut-away model to
contain call number
title and property
stamp

FIGURE 30. CUT-AWAY MODEL

Label model and all removable parts.

For protection use cardboard boxes properly labeled, or polyethylene bags which may be obtained in a variety of sizes and enable the user to see the three-dimensional representation without opening the container.

MOTION PICTURE FILMS

MOTION PICTURE FILM FORMATS

The film formats most commonly used in libraries and homes are the 16mm and the 8mm. Films in other widths are for special purposes: 35mm for commercial theatrical motion pictures; 55mm (Cinemascope) and 70mm (Todd-AO) for wide screen effects.

16 mm FILMS

SYMBOL: MP   COLOR CODE: BLUE

Both silent and sound 16mm films may be purchased, rented, or obtained on free loan. A silent film has sprocket holes on both edges and projects at a speed of 16 frames per second. A sound film has sprocket holes only on one edge and projects at a speed of 24 frames per second.

FILM EVALUATION

Valuable information on film selection will be found in:

Jones, Emily S. *Manual on Film Evaluation*. New York: Educational Film Library Association, 1967.

These publications provide evaluative reviews up-dated by frequent and/or regular periodic issues:

The Booklist (Formerly *Booklist and Subscription Books Bulletin*). American Library Association, 50 E. Huron St., Chicago, Ill. 60611. Semi-monthly. $10.
Film reviews are compiled quarterly by the ALA Audio-Visual Committee's Film Review Subcommittee. Suggestions are given on the various ways the film may be used and on its value for the public library collection. Highly technical and specifically curriculum-oriented films are not included. This quarterly compilation will continue until 16mm film is assimilated into the semi-monthly nonprint media reviewing program (see Chapter 3). Supplements *Films for Libraries* (1962), a compilation of selected *Booklist* reviews.

EFLA Evaluations. Educational Film Library Association, Inc., 250 W. 57th St., New York, N.Y. 10019. Monthly. $15 (Membership), plus service-basis charge depending on size of film library.
Film evaluations, printed on 3"x5" cards, include general rating, technical rating, annotation, and the appeal and importance of the film. The *Film Evalua-*

tion Guide, 1946–64 and the *1964–67 Supplement* presents a selected compilation of these reviews to August, 1967.

Film Review Digest. Educational Film Library Association, Inc., 250 W. 57th St., New York, N.Y. 10019. 8/yr. $4.

Descriptive and evaluative excerpts from three or more sources for about a dozen 16mm films in each issue.

Films in Review. National Board of Review of Motion Pictures, 31 Union Square West, New York, N.Y. 10005. 10/yr. $6.

Landers Film Reviews. Landers Associates, P.O. Box 69760, Los Angeles, Calif. 90069. 10/yr. $30.

Descriptive and evaluative reviews give comprehensive coverage of non-theatrical releases, including foreign films. Cumulated indexes are provided for each volume.

See also, *Audiovisual Instruction, Educational Screen & Audiovisual Guide,* and *Film News,* all discussed in Chapter 3.

CATALOGING

COLLATION   Running time, sound or silent, color statement, width in milli-meters. (A full reel contains 560 feet of film. The running time of a full reel of 16mm sound film is 10 minutes. Add one third for the running time of silent film.)

```
MP
027.62     The pleasure is mutual: how to conduct effective
P1             picture book programs, prepared by Joanna
           Foster and William D. Stoneback.  Motion pic-
           ture.  Westchester Library System, N.Y.,
           1966.
           24 min., sd., color, 16mm.

           Intended to help librarians, teachers, and
           volunteers in storytelling and introducing new
           books to children.

           LIBRARY SERVICE/ PICTURE BOOKS FOR CHILDREN/
           STORYTELLING
```

16mm film.

Dewey Decimal classification system.

Optional: Added entries for these responsible for preparation, producer.

MP
1630   In search of Medea: the art of Sylvia Lefkowitz.
                    Motion picture. National Film Board of Cana-
                    da, 1966.
                    14 min., sd., color, 16mm.

                    Recounts how the Canadian sculptress went to
                    Greece to discover Medea and later recreated her
                    in bronze.

                    LEFKOWITZ, SYLVIA/ SCULPTURE

16mm film.
Accession classification system.
Optional: Added entry for producer.

PHYSICAL PROCESSING

Label leader of film, reel, and edge of film can lid. If "head" and "tail" leaders, preprinted with the name of the library, are used, splice six to eight feet of these to the beginning and end of the film and write in call number.

The circulation card may be kept in the can or at the desk.

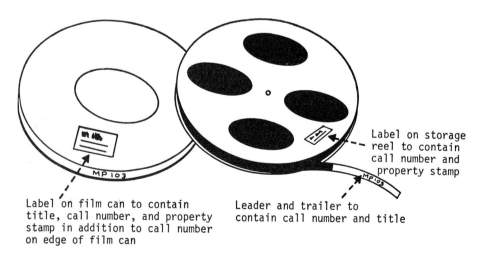

Label on film can to contain   Leader and trailer to
title, call number, and property   contain call number and title
stamp in addition to call number
on edge of film can

Label on storage
reel to contain
call number and
property stamp

FIGURE 31. 16MM MOTION PICTURE FILM

8mm FILMS

SYMBOL: ML   COLOR CODE: BLUE

DEFINITION   Silent or sound films, available in film loops contained in a cartridge or in reel-to-reel packaging. Those which treat only one subject are sometimes called single-concept films and usually have a running time of 5 minutes or less. Longer 8mm feature films are now gaining in popularity. Currently, the three different formats of 8mm films most widely used are:

Standard 8. The original format used, with large sprocket holes, sound track optional. This is sometimes referred to as Regular 8.

Super 8. This format has a reduced size sprocket hole which permits an increased picture area.

Super Sound 8. The sound track, magnetic or optical, is placed in a position opposite to that used with Standard 8.

Compatibility of projector and cartridge must be checked since all 8mm formats cannot be projected on the same equipment. In addition, unless orders for 8mm films specifically state the format desired, the vendor will usually supply a Standard 8 film.

Research on 8mm films and equipment is continuous and changes are rapid. Hopefully, a standardization of projectors and cartridges will eventually be reached. Meanwhile, the 8mm film is becoming more and more popular since it is particularly adaptable to individual use both in the library and in the home.

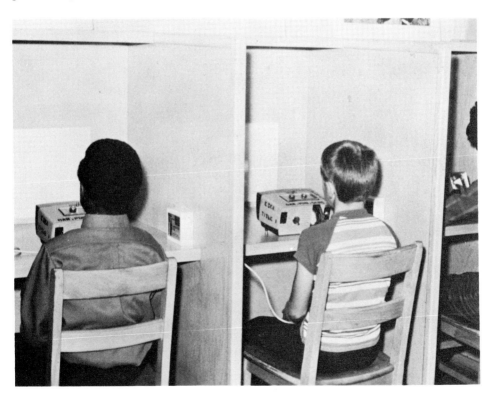

FIGURE 32. INDIVIDUAL USE OF 8MM FILM. *8mm film is becoming more and more popular, because it is particularly suitable for individual use in the library.* (Photograph courtesy of Oakland, California, Public Schools.)

CATALOGING

COLLATION   Running time to nearest minute, sound or silent, color statement, width in millimeters, format.

ADDITIONAL INFORMATION AFTER COLLATION   Accompanying material or attached notes. Type of projector needed.

```
ML
599        Common native animals.  Motion picture.  Chand-
Co             ler, 1967.
               3½ min., si., color, 8mm film loop mounted
           in cartridge.  Let's see the animals.
               Teaching guide in cartridge case.
              —Use with Technicolor instant movie projector.

               Shows habits and physical characteristics of
           the fox, skunk, raccoon, coyote, and peccary.

           ANIMALS- HABITS AND BEHAVIOR/ MAMMALS/ ser
```

8mm film.
Dewey Decimal classification system.
Collation: super 8mm. if film is in this format.

OPTIONAL   After title: statement of credit for making film.
Notes: statement of material from which film is adapted, e.g., Adapted from the
    1961 16mm sound motion picture entitled *Title*.
Credits: educational author, director, dissector, conductor, etc.
Added entries: series, producer, names of film maker, director, etc.

```
ML
6104-06    Frog egg.  Motion picture.  Educational Services.
              Ealing Corp., 1967.
              3 film loops, 4 min. each, si., color, 8mm,
           mounted in cartridge.
              Notes on cartridge case.
              Use with Technicolor instant movie projector.

              Part 1: First cell division to early neural
           fold.- Part 2: Development of the body regions.-
           Part 3: Continued development to hatching.
              Uses time-lapse photography to record the
                                      (Cont'd. on next card)
```

8mm films in a series cataloged as one set.
Accession classification system.
Continuation card necessary.

```
ML                                            Card 2
6104-06    Frog egg.

           development of a single frog egg over a period
           of about five days.




           EMBRYOLOGY- FROGS
```

Continuation card for 8mm films in a series cataloged as one set.

The statement of running time, if it varies for each film loop, may be omitted from the collation and added after the title of each film in the contents note, e.g., Part 1: First cell division to early neural fold, 4 min.

IDENTIFYING CALL NUMBER FOR EACH FILM LOOP IN SET   If accession classification system is used, consecutive numbers are assigned to each film in the set.

If Dewey Decimal classification system is used, the number of each film, preceded by a dash, may be added after the letters below the classification number, e.g., ML 597 Fr-3, or the designation v.1, v.2, etc. may be placed below the letters, e.g., ML 597 Fr v.3.

If the library wishes to check out each film loop separately, the call number on the circulation card for each film should show this individual film number.

Optional: title added entries may be made for each film loop.

```
ML
6104-06    Frog egg.  Motion picture.  Educational Services.
              Ealing Corp., 1967.
              3 film loops, 4 min. each, si., color, 8mm,
           mounted in cartridge.
              Notes on cartridge case.

           88-420  Jack Ford  10/3/67  45.50

6104       Part 1: First cell division to early neural fold.
6104 c.2      "


                              (Cont'd. on next card)
```

8mm films in a series cataloged as one set.
Shelf-list card.
Duplicate copy in accession classification system.

OPTIONAL   The accession number of each title in the series may be listed as shown, or purchase information only may be given.

```
                                   Card 2
ML
6104-06    Frog egg.

6105       Part 2: Development of the body regions.
6105 c.2      "
6106       Part 3: Continued development to hatching.
6106 c.2    .."
```

Shelf-list continuation card for films (8mm) in a series cataloged as one set.

PHYSICAL PROCESSING

Label cartridge and spine of packaging case with ownership and call number. Provide title label if necessary.

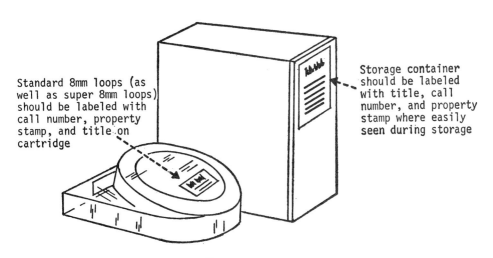

Standard 8mm loops (as well as super 8mm loops) should be labeled with call number, property stamp, and title on cartridge

Storage container should be labeled with title, call number, and property stamp where easily seen during storage

FIGURE 33. 8MM FILM LOOPS

SOURCES OF INFORMATION

8: Newsletter of 8mm Film in Education. Project in Educational Communication, Horace Mann-Lincoln Institute of School Experimentation, Teachers College, Columbia University, New York, N.Y. 10027. Issued irregularly. Request.

Evaluative reviews of new commercial and noncommercial film loops and research reports on new equipment and techniques.

Kone, Grace Ann, ed. *8mm Film Directory.* Educational Film Library Association, Inc. Distributed by Comprehensive Service Corporation, 250 W. 64th St., New York, N.Y. 10023. 1969.

Lists more than 5,000 films in all formats, arranged by subject matter, with descriptions and Dewey Decimal number, with an alphabetical index and Dewey Decimal index. A directory of producers and distributors, and a pictorial guide to the various types of 8mm projectors now in use are also included. The EFLA magazine *Sightlines* will carry supplements to the Directory.

Sound Film Loop Source Directory, 1968; *Source Directory: Educational Single-Concept Films*, 4th ed., 1967. Technicolor, Inc., Commercial and Educational Division, 1300 Frawley Drive, Costa Mesa, Calif. 92627.

PICTURES
SYMBOL: PP   COLOR CODE: SALMON

DEFINITION   Included here are posters, post cards, cartoons, photographs, and facsimile reproductions of documents. For drawings, paintings, and print reproductions of other works of art, see the "Art Prints" section.

ACQUISITION

Pictures are readily available, either free or at a low cost, in great quantity and varying quality. The numerous sources for obtaining pictures include commercial organizations, photography companies, tourist agencies, state and federal agencies, magazines, local stores and newsstands. Three very helpful pamphlets which list sources are: *Sources of Free Pictures, Sources of Inexpensive Pictures,* and *Sources of Free Travel Posters* (Bruce Miller Publications, Box 369, Riverside, Calif. 92502).

CATALOGING

COLLATION   Number, type of picture (e.g., photographs, posters, postcards, etc.), dimensions, color statement, special format.

```
PP
979.49    Los Angeles is ... by Everett B. Chaffee.  Pic-
Lo            ture.   Day, 1965.
            24 photographs, 18"x18", b&w, wire bound.
        Urban education studies.   Special city albums.
            Teaching guide.

            Portrays life in a large California city and
        helps develop relationships to the larger world.


        CITY LIFE/ LOS ANGELES, CALIFORNIA/ ser
```

Set of pictures.
Dewey Decimal classification system.

PHYSICAL PROCESSING

UNMOUNTED PICTURES   Treat these as vertical file material. Assign subject heading and place in filing envelope or folder labeled with corresponding subject heading (see Vertical File Materials section).

MOUNTED PICTURES   (see Charts section for methods of mounting and processing).

Mounting materials: Cover-paper in warm tones of gray or tan, in the weight used to cover small pamphlets, in 9"x12" and 12"x18" sizes, makes the least expensive and most serviceable mount. This is available from most paper manufacturing companies. Heavy mounting paper is available from library supply dealers. Standard white or off-white mounting board is rigid and durable, available in standard sizes. It is somewhat expensive and soils easily.

Protective coatings: A variety of coatings are available, the least expensive being plastic spray and plastic bags. Another type, somewhat more expensive, consists of plastic "envelopes" where the picture slides between two sheets of transparent plastic. Available from library supply houses, these provide excellent protection, but are shiny and apt to produce a glare that is unsatisfactory for viewing.

Plastic lamination, using a laminating machine, is a fourth method, obviously an expensive one, and would be restricted to those libraries where the volume of pictures processed is large enough to justify the expense involved in purchasing the machinery.

POSTCARDS For individual study or for use in the opaque projector, postcards may be placed uniformly on mounts large enough to insure proper placement during projection, labeled, and filed in vertical file, shoe box, or wooden box.

BIBLIOGRAPHY

Ireland,, Norma O. *The Picture File in School, College, and Public Libraries.* Boston: F. W. Faxon, 1952.

Miller, Bruce. *So You Want to Start a Picture File.* Riverside, Calif.: The author, 1954.

Williams, Catharine M. *Learning from Pictures.* 2d ed. Washington, D.C.: N.E.A. Dept. of Audiovisual Instruction, 1968.

PROGRAMMED INSTRUCTION
SYMBOL: KP   COLOR CODE: BLACK STRIP

DEFINITION An autoinstructional device that presents information in logical step-by-step sequences, permitting a person to test himself and proceed to the next segment at his own ability rate. Programmed instruction is available in several different forms and may include print and nonprint media in various combinations.

SELECTION SOURCES

These compilations list and describe available programs:

NSPI Journal. National Society for Programmed Instruction, Trinity University, 715 Stadium Dr., San Antonio, Tex. 78212. 10/yr. Membership ($7.50 for nonmembers).

Programmed Instruction: An International Directory, compiled under the direction of Seth Spaulding. International Education Clearing House, School of Education, Univ. of Pittsburgh, Pittsburgh, Pa. 15213, 1967.

Programmed Instruction Guide, 2nd ed. Entelek, Inc., 42 Pleasant St., Newbury-port, Mass. 01950, 1968.

Programed Instruction, K-6. Product Information Supplement #1, *Educational Product Report* 2, No. 1 (Oct. 1968).

Programed Instruction, 7-12. Product Information Supplement #6, *Educational Product Report* 2, No. 6 (Mar. 1969).

Programed Learning: A Bibliography of Programs and Presentation Devices, 4th ed., compiled by Dr. Carl Hendershot. 4114 Ridgewood Drive, Bay City, Mich. 48706, 1967–68. Has 1967, 1968 supplements.

CATALOGING

COLLATION Number of frames, format, expected completion time (usually stated by the publisher). Optional: Dimensions of frames.

SERIES NOTE For well-known series, e.g., TEMAC, Tutor Texts.

GRADE LEVEL After series note, or after collation if series is not stated.

NOTES Specify equipment necessary for use (e.g., use with MTA Teaching Machine); basic program type: linear, branching, or mixed construction, and whether or not it is designed to be written in; any other special information or description needed to use material.

ADDED ENTRY Make an added entry for organization or corporation which authored the program.

```
KP
550      Geology.  Programmed instruction.    EBE, 1964.
Ge            1,101 fr., book, 14-35 hrs.    6.
              Teachers manual; Test booklet.

              A linear program covering scientific method,
         weathering, erosion, rock classification, de-
         position and uplift, interior of the earth, the
         earth's crust.


         GEOLOGY/ Encyclopaedia Britannica Educational
         Corporation
```

Programmed instruction.
Dewey Decimal classification system.
Book format.

```
KP
568        The age of dinosaurs.  Programmed instruction.
Ag             Honor Products Co., 1962.
               200 fr., roll, 3 hrs.   4.
               Teachers guide; Pre- and post-tests.

               Use in Honor Teaching Machine.  A program of
           mixed construction, intended for enrichment.
           Names and physical characteristics, eating and
           living habits of prehistoric animals are covered.

           DINOSAURS/ Honor Products Company
```

Programmed instruction.
Dewey Decimal classification system.
Machine format.

PHYSICAL PROCESSING

Label ownership and call number in most suitable position according to the format of the material. Accompanying material or equipment which is specifically included in the programmed instruction packet carries the same call number.

If necessary, a list of all parts may be pasted in.

BIBLIOGRAPHY

Gee, Ralph D. "Agorithmic Mathetical Reinforcement: The Implications of Programmed Instruction for the Librarian." *Library Association Record* 67 (Jul. 1965): 228–52.

National Society for the Study of Education. Committee on Programed Instruction. *Programed Instruction.* 66th Yearbook, part 2. Ed. by Phil C. Lange. Chicago: University of Chicago Press, 1967.

Ofiesh, Gabriel D., and Wesley C. Meierhenry, eds. *Trends in Programmed Instruction: Papers from the First Annual Convention of the National Society for Programmed Instruction.* Published for the Dept. of Audiovisual Instruction, NEA, and the National Society for Programmed Instruction. Washington, D.C.: National Education Association, 1964.

Ryan, William F. *A Handbook of Programed Learning Information.* Albany, N.Y.: University of the State of New York, 1964.

Wehl, Seth F. "Pointers on the Purchase and Use of PI." *Educational Product Report* 2, No. 1 (Oct. 1968): 14–17.

REALIA
SYMBOL: DS   COLOR CODE: BROWN STRIP

DEFINITION   Real objects. In a teaching-learning situation they are used to relate instruction to real life.

CATALOGING

COLLATION   Dimensions or size, if applicable.
NOTES   Further necessary physical description.

```
DS
25        Fuse box.  Realia.    Cutler-Hammer, 1967.
             10"x18"x3".
             Wiring manual.

          A wall-mounted fuse box showing the basic
          wiring system.  Inside the door is a wiring
          diagram to be used with instruction manual.



          ELECTRIC WIRING
```

---

*Realia.
Accession classification system.

PHYSICAL PROCESSING

Tie on any removable parts. Label object, parts, and container.

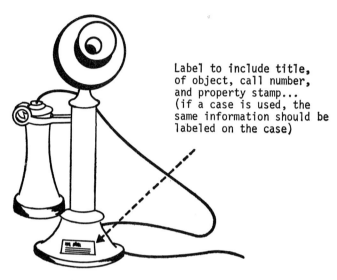

Label to include title,
of object, call number,
and property stamp...
(if a case is used, the
same information should be
labeled on the case)

FIGURE 34. REALIA

RECORDINGS, DISC
SYMBOL: RD   COLOR CODE: CHERRY

Records are produced in diameters of 7″, 10″, 12″ and 16″, and at playback speeds of 45, 78, 33⅓, and 16⅔ revolutions per minute. Currently, the most commonly used is the 33.3 rpm. microgroove monophonic (monaural) and stereophonic recording.

The phonograph or record player provided for playback must accommodate both the speed and the audio technique (monophonic or stereophonic) of the record. A stereo cartridge will play both mono and stereo records, but a mono cartridge will damage a stereo record.

CATALOGING

IDENTIFICATION OF MATERIAL   Record, disc; Recording, disc; Phonorecord; Phonodisc; or, Audiodisc.

COLLATION   Number of sides, diameter in inches, revolutions per minute, stereo (where applicable). To eliminate the difficulty of typing 33⅓, use 33.3 rpm.

NOTES Specify the performing medium (vocal, instrumental, piano, guitar) and type of presentation (dramatization, narration, reading) if this information is not given after the title.

OPTIONAL

IMPRINT Where title similarities occur confusion will be minimized by using the publisher's record number for identification. This is taken from the record label or jacket and is stated after the publisher's name.

COLLATION Number of records is noted before the number of sides, e.g., 3 records, 6s.
Running time is noted after revolutions per minute, e.g., 33.3 rpm., 9 min.
Mono, for monaural, is designated after revolutions per minute. This is not essential since monaural records may be played on all types of equipment. Stereo recordings, however, must always be noted.

ACCOMPANYING MATERIAL Number of pages of descriptive notes, e.g., script (6 p.) in slipcase.

NOTES Credits to persons and/or groups involved in the performance and/or production.
Complete contents for all bands or parts of each side of the record.

TRACINGS Added entries for all the above if necessary.

```
RD
1432        Anthology of Negro poets.  Record, disc.  Ed. by
              Arna Bontemps.   Folkways, 1961.
              2s, 12", 33.3 rpm.
              Biography of poets in slipcase.

              Six Negro poets read from their own works:
            Langston Hughes, Sterling Brown, Claude McKay,
            Countee Cullen, Gwendolyn Brooks, Margaret
            Walker.


            NEGRO POETRY/ POETRY- COLLECTIONS
```

Single record.
Collection of spoken material read by several people.
Accession classification system.
Optional: Listing of poem titles; added entries for poems, poets, editor.

```
RD
822.3        The taming of the shrew, by William Shakespeare.
Ta               Record, disc.   Folkways, 1966.
             4s, 12", 33.3 rpm.
             Notes on the performing company and text.

             Recorded during a performance of the Shake-
             speare for Students Company.



             COMEDY/ Shakespeare, William
```

Record album.
Literary work.
Dewey Decimal classification system.
Title main entry.

```
RD
822.3        Shakespeare's The taming of the shrew.   Record,
Sh               disc.   Folkways, 1966.
             4s, 12", 33.3 rpm.
             Notes on the performing company and text.

             Recorded during a performance of the Shake-
             speare for Students Company.



             COMEDY/ Shakespeare, William/ t: The taming of
             the shrew.
```

Record album.
Literary work.
Dewey Decimal classification system.
Filing title main entry, using possessive form of author's name as first word of title.

```
RD
822.3      Shakespeare, William
Sh             The taming of the shrew.  Record, disc.
           Folkways, 1966.
               4s, 12", 33.3 rpm.
               Notes on the performing company and text.

               Recorded during a performance of the Shake-
           speare for Students Company.


           COMEDY/ t
```

Record album.
Literary work.
Dewey Decimal classification system.
Author main entry.
Optional: Added entry for performing company.

```
RD
785        Mahler's Symphony no. 7 (Song of the night).
Ma             Record, disc.   Vanguard, 1965.
               4s, 12", 33.3 rpm.   Vanguard recordings for
           the conoisseur.
               Program notes bound-in.

               Utah Symphony Orchestra, Maurice Abravanel,
           conductor.


           SYMPHONIES/ Mahler, Gustav/ t: Song of the
           night.
```

Record album.
Music.
Dewey Decimal classification system.
Filing title main entry, using possessive form of composer's name as beginning
    title word.
Optional: Added entries for orchestra and conductor.

```
RD
1725        Holiday for strings.  Record, disc.  RCA Victor,
               1966.
            2s, 12", 33.3 rpm., stereo.
            Program notes on slipcase.

            Boston Pops Orchestra, Arthur Fiedler, con-
            ductor.  Contains original works and arrange-
            ments.


            STRING-ORCHESTRA MUSIC/ Boston Pops Orchestra/
            Fiedler, Arthur
```

Record album.
Music. A collection of several composer's works.
Accession classification system.
Optional: Added entries for orchestra and conductor.

```
RD
784         Children's songs of Mexico.  Record, disc.  Bow-
Ch             mar, 1965.
               2s, 12", 33.3 rpm.
               Text & descriptive notes; 2 fs: 29, 32 fr.,
            color.

               Filmstrips correlated with record to provide
            words, notation, and pictures descriptive of the
            Mexican custom each song represents.

            FOLK SONGS, MEXICAN/ MEXICO
```

Single record with accompanying material.
Dewey Decimal classification system.
Text and filmstrips have same call number and symbol as record. See also example
   under Kits.

```
RD
Wa        Walt Disney's Peter Pan.  Record, disc.  Based
             on the story by Sir James M. Barrie, adapted
             from the motion picture.  RCA Victor, 1952.
             4s, 7", 45 rpm.
             Script and illustrations spiral bound-in.

          Narration interspersed with songs.


          FAIRY TALES/ Barrie, James M./ Disney (Walt)
          Productions/ t: Peter Pan.
```

Record album.
Narration and music.
Classified as fiction.

PHYSICAL PROCESSING

Adhere label with call number and ownership identification to record label on both sides of the record so that it does not cover pertinent information. A special half-round or crescent label is not necessary. The $1\frac{1}{2}''$x1″ pressure sensitive label can easily be fitted on the majority of records without covering essential printing. The call number is typed in the $\frac{5}{8}''$ remaining below the preprinted library name.

FIGURE 35. RECORD WITH LABEL

Label each record within an album with album call number and the sequence number of the record.

If the record does not specify the revolutions per minute, this information should be clearly marked on the record label on both sides of the record. Many 78 rpm. records are not so designated by the manufacturer.

Stereo should also be noted if it does not appear on the record. To alert the patron to the necessity of using stereophonic equipment, commercially available 'Stereo' imprinted labels may be applied to all stereo records.

If the title on the slipcase differs from that on the record, a title label showing the title main entry under which the work has been cataloged should be placed above the printed title on the slipcase or record so that the two conform.

If the work has been cataloged under a supplied (e.g., possessive of the composer's name) or conventional title, this title should be labeled above the printed title on the slipcase and on both sides of all records.

For protection use plastic or pressboard record holders, available from library supply houses. If needed, additional sleeves to hold records may be inserted, using adhesive cloth or mystic tape. Mylar slip covers provide additional protection for albums and single records.

Label outside of record holder in upper left corner of the front and upper right corner of the back. On this label include the total number of records in an album. If desired, a contents note may be added. The call number may also be lettered or labeled on the spine of an album.

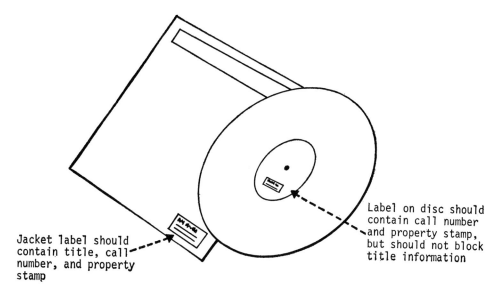

Jacket label should contain title, call number, and property stamp

Label on disc should contain call number and property stamp, but should not block title information

FIGURE 36. DISC RECORDINGS

The circulation card should note the number of records, if more than one. A pocket and Date Due form may be pasted on the inside or outside of the front cover of the record holder.

Records should be stored in an upright position, on shelves, or in specially designed cabinets or browser bins.

BIBLIOGRAPHY

Barnes, Christopher. "Classification and Cataloging of Spoken Records in Academic Libraries." *College & Research Libraries* 28, No. 1 (Jan. 1967): 49–52.

Hagist, Barbara. "Resistance and Reluctance in Record Selection." *Library Journal* 93, No. 3 (Feb. 1, 1968): 518–20.

Kujoth, Jean S., ed. *Readings in Nonbook Librarianship*. Metuchen, N.J.: Scarecrow Press, 1968.

Lissner, John. "Pop/Folk/Jazz; Guideposts to a Basic Record Library." *Library Journal* 94, No. 2 (Jan. 15, 1969): 158–61.

Pearson, Mary D. *Recordings in the Public Library*. Chicago: American Library Association, 1963.

SLIDES
SYMBOL: TS　　COLOR CODE: BUFF

DEFINITION　A single picture on film or transparent material bound or masked to a 2"x2", 2¼"x2¼", or 3¼"x4" "frame" for viewing through a slide viewer or projector.

Because of its evident physical advantages the 35mm film 2"x2" slide has replaced the 3¼"x4" lantern slide. However, the glass slide is still in use for special subject, specimen and silhouette slides prepared locally. Currently, both 3¼"x4" and 2¼"x2¼" photographic slides are available through the use of Polaroid Land projection film.

Slides carrying their own sound are also being developed. A separate accompanying recording is no longer necessary, because each slide has, mounted on its frame, a tape recording that provides sound for a specified time, also permitting erasure and re-recording, if desired.

At present, a choice of slide projectors in a wide range of sizes and costs may be made from hand-operated, cartridge-fed, and remote control models. Again, it is advisable to check compatibility of slides and equipment since many projectors will not take glass slides, and automatic models may jam if the slide mount is of plastic, metal, or tape binding, instead of cardboard. The sound-on-slide system also requires a special projector-recorder.

CATALOGING

Commercial slides are usually packaged in sets. If further subject division seems warranted, the set may be split and cataloged as individual slides and/or several small sets.

COLLATION　Number of slides, size, color statement. If slide is made of anything other than film, or if the frame carries a tape recording, this should be noted.

ACCOMPANYING MATERIAL　A narration recorded on disc or tape may be provided. Treat the same as accompanying material for filmstrips.

OPTIONAL NOTES　Source of photographs, photographer.

```
TS
709.38      Art of Greece.  Slide.  Sandak, 1968.
Ar              30 slides, 2"x2", color.

                Renowned treasures of architecture and sculp-
            ture, from archaic through Hellenistic Greece.



            ART, GREEK
```

Set of slides.
Dewey Decimal classification system.

PHYSICAL PROCESSING

To position the label, turn the slide so that the picture is upside down, with the glossy side of the film toward you. Place the label on the upper right half of the slide. This is the corner by which the slide is held when it is put into the projector.

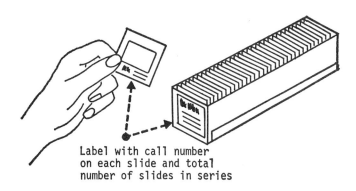

Label with call number
on each slide and total
number of slides in series

FIGURE 37. 2x2 SLIDES

This label carries the call number for individual slides, the set call number and individual slide number for each slide in a set. Ownership may be stamped on the label or on the frame of the slide below the label. Label the set container.

Slides may be filed in boxes of various sizes supplied by camera shops, stored in cartridges which fit projectors, or placed in appropriately labeled envelopes and filed in regular vertical file cabinets. If sets and individual slides are stored in plastic pocket sheets it is easy to see 25 slides at a time against a slide sorter. Specially designed cabinets with slide drawers are available, as are vertical display racks which allow visual scanning of up to 120 slides at one time.

SPECIMENS
SYMBOL: DS   COLOR CODE: BROWN STRIP

DEFINITION   A part or sample of a real object.

CATALOGING

TITLE   If no title appears on the specimen, the mount, the box, or the teaching guide or explanatory notes, a title is supplied which identifies the specimen, e.g., Butterflies of the Monterey Peninsula; Seashell collection.

COLLATION   Number of specimens if more than one.

OPTIONAL   Contents note.

```
DS
595.7     Seven insect types.   Specimen.   Denoyer-Gep-
Se             pert.
               7 specimens imbedded in plastic.

               Silverfish, grasshopper, squashbug, Japanese
          beetle, cabbage butterfly, honeybee, housefly.



          INSECTS
```

Set of specimens.
Dewey Decimal classification system.

PHYSICAL PROCESSING

Label specimens and container. If several individual specimens are packaged together each specimen should be labeled, and an inventory of the contents pasted inside the lid of the box.

Specimen should be labeled
with call number, title, and
property stamp

FIGURE 38. SPECIMEN IN PLASTIC

STUDY PRINTS
SYMBOL: PS   COLOR CODE: SALMON

DEFINITION A picture dealing with a specific subject. Study prints are usually prepared in a set portraying different aspects and development of a subject.

CATALOGING

COLLATION Number of prints if more than one (mounted or unmounted), dimensions, color statement, and special format.

```
PS
301        Neighborhood friends and helpers.  Study print.
Ne             SVE, 1966.
           8 mounted prints, 18"x13", color.
           Teaching guide and text on reverse of prints.

           Portrays various occupations and services in
           a community.  May be used with filmstrips,
           slides and text materials.  All grade levels.


           COMMUNITY LIFE/ OCCUPATIONS
```

Set of study prints.
Dewey Decimal classification system.

PHYSICAL PROCESSING

Study prints are processed in the same manner as art prints, charts, and pictures.

TAPE RECORDINGS
SYMBOL: RT   COLOR CODE: CHERRY

DEFINITION   A magnetic tape having a dull and shiny side, on which sound is recorded. Only the dull side carries the recording.

TAPE FORMATS

Tapes are available in several formats and speeds, pre-recorded or blank.

OPEN REEL TAPES   The standard tape width is ¼", on reels of 3, 5, and 7 inches. Recordings for general use are made at speeds of 1⅞, 3¾, and 7½ inches per second.

CASSETTE TAPES   The standard tape width is ⅛". The tape is enclosed in a cassette, or sealed container, which fits into position on the recorder, thus eliminating the necessity for manual threading. To play the second track, or side, the cassette is flipped over. Cassettes play at a speed of 1⅞ inches per second and may be procured in lengths for 10, 20, 30, 40, 60, 90 or 120 minutes. Because of their compactness and ease of threading, it is anticipated that cassettes may become more popular than reel-to-reel tapes.

CARTRIDGE OR LOOP TAPES   The ends of the tape are joined together to form an endless loop, thus providing continuous playback without rewinding. Available in four and eight tracks, cartridge tapes are often used in automobiles, and in commercial advertising where a repetitive recorded message is needed.

RECORDING MODES

MONAURAL, SINGLE TRACK, FULL TRACK   The recording covers the full width of the dull side of the tape.

DUAL TRACK, TWO-TRACK, HALF-TRACK MONAURAL   A recording is made in opposite directions on each half of the dull side of the tape. To use the second track the reel need only be turned over, with no rewinding necessary.

TWO-TRACK STEREO, HALF-TRACK STEREO   Two separate parallel tracks are recorded, both in the same direction. Rewinding is necessary before the tape can be replayed.

FOUR MONAURAL TRACKS, QUARTER-TRACK   Four separate tracks are recorded, one at a time, on one side of the tape. The first and third tracks are recorded in one direction, the second and fourth in the opposite direction.

FOUR-TRACK STEREO   The first and third tracks are recorded in pairs running in one direction, the second and fourth simultaneously in the other direction.

Eight-track tapes are now being used more widely, especially for broadcasting and commercial purposes.

RECORDING TIME

Recording time is determined by the tape length and the recorder speed. The longer the tape, the longer the playing time; the slower the speed, the longer the playing time. The number of feet of tape on a reel will vary with the thickness of the tape. A full 5″ reel usually holds 600 feet, but can accommodate 1200 feet of special base extra long play tape; a 7″ reel holds 1200 feet, but can take 3600 feet of special base tape.

For quick reference, the following chart gives recording times for the most commonly used lengths and speeds, for single track mono or two-track stereo tapes. The time should be doubled for two-track mono or four-track stereo, and quadrupled for four-track mono tapes.

TAPE RECORDING TIME			
Tape Length	1 ⅞ ips.	3.75 ips.	7.5 ips.
150 ft.	15 min.	7½ min.	3.75 min.
225 ft.	24 min.	12 min.	6 min.
300 ft.	30 min.	15 min.	7½ min.
600 ft.	1 hr.	30 min.	15 min.
900 ft.	1½ hrs.	45 min.	22½ min.
1200 ft.	2 hrs.	1 hr.	30 min.
1800 ft.	3 hrs.	1½ hrs.	45 min.
2400 ft.	4 hrs.	2 hrs.	1 hr.
3600 ft.	6 hrs.	3 hrs.	1½ hrs.

TABLE 3. TAPE RECORDING TIMES

CATALOGING

IDENTIFICATION OF MATERIAL   Record, tape; Recording, tape; Phono-tape; or, Audio-tape.

COLLATION   Number of reels if more than 1, running time in minutes, speed in inches per second (ips.), number of tracks if more than one, stereo (where applicable). Cassette, or cartridge, replaces number of reels if tape is in this format.

OPTIONAL   Size of reel, 3″, 5″, 7″; Single track; Mono.

RT
979.4
Ca
    The California gold rush. Record, tape. Wo-
       men's Auxiliary of Veterans of Foreign Wars.
       15 min., $7\frac{1}{2}$ ips.   The American trail.

       Bing Crosby and his son, Lindsay, narrate the
    story of Tom Brooks, a gold rush enthusiast, and
    his organization of a vigilante committee to re-
    store law and order.

    CALIFORNIA- GOLD DISCOVERIES

Tape recording.
Dewey Decimal classification system.
Title main entry.
Optional: Added entries for narrators, series.

RT
3684
    Cool jazz. Record, tape. Radio Station, Iowa
       State University, 1961.
       30 min., 3.75 ips.   Roots of jazz.

       Features quotes from jazz experts, personal
    interviews with jazz musicians, and musical ex-
    cerpts.

    JAZZ MUSIC/ ser

Tape recording.
Narration and music.
Accession classification system.
Optional: Added entry for producer.

PHYSICAL PROCESSING

Label leader, or splice 3 feet of plastic or Mylar white leader to "head" and "tail," and label. This will avoid confusion should the tape be rewound on the wrong reel.

Label on edge of storage box with call number visible when stored on shelf

Labels on tape storage boxes include call number and title

Label on tape reel to match call number on box

FIGURE 39. AUDIO TAPES

Label call number, ownership, and title, if necessary, on reel or cassette. These labels may be placed where space permits, but consistency in their position should be maintained as far as possible. On reels, if the information is not supplied, label the speed, number of tracks, and stereo (if applicable).

On spine of container, label title, call number, ownership. If desired, additional information may be typed on a label and pasted on the face or inside the lid of the container: playing time, speed, number of tracks, stereo. Depending upon the visibility permitted by the storage facilities, label cassette containers on the edge or the lid.

The circulation card may be laid in the container, placed in a pocket pasted on one face of the container, or kept at the desk.

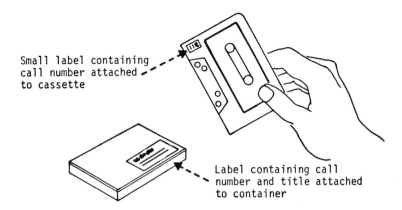

Small label containing call number attached to cassette

Label containing call number and title attached to container

FIGURE 40. AUDIO CASSETTE

SOURCES OF INFORMATION

Harrison Catalog of Stereophonic Tapes. 274 Madison Ave., New York, N.Y. 10016. 5/yr.

National Audio Tape Catalog. Boulder, Colo.: National Center for Audio Tapes, University of Colorado. Annual. $3.

Phonolog Tape Parade. Phonolog Publishing Co., 2720 Beverly Blvd., Los Angeles, Calif. 90057. Monthly. Supplemented by *Phonolog List-o-Tapes,* issued quarterly.

Tape Recording. Eastern News Distributors, Inc., 155 W. 15th St., New York, N.Y. 10011. Bimonthly, except monthly in November and December. Descriptive-evaluative reviews of tape-recorded classical and popular music, with ratings for music, performance, and quality of recording.

TRANSPARENCIES
SYMBOL: TR   COLOR CODE: BUFF

DEFINITION   An image on transparent material which is enlarged through the use of an overhead projector. It is usually 7"x7" or 10"x10". Transparencies are frequently made with one or more overlays, which are additional transparent sheets with lettering or other matter designed to fit over the base transparency in order to supplement the initial information and show conceptual relationships.

The introduction of motion increases and broadens the concepts that can be presented by transparencies. A mechanism is provided for manipulation so that the projected picture shows movement. Transparencies need not be limited by the overhead projector to group use. Compact, portable equipment, designed for individual transparency viewing, is now being produced.

CATALOGING

COLLATION   Total number of transparencies, mounted or unmounted, or one transparency with number of overlays, dimensions, color statement.

OPTIONAL CONTENTS NOTE   Titles of individual transparencies in a set, each followed by the number of overlays, where applicable; titles of subject units in a set with number of transparencies in each unit.

```
TR
612        Circulatory system.  Transparency.  General
Ci             Aniline & Film, 1961.
               1 transparency with 1 overlay, 10"x10",
           color. General science projecto aid.    4-9.


               The use of the overlay gives a clear picture
           of the anatomical structure of the circulatory
           system.


           BLOOD- CIRCULATION/ ser
```

Single transparency with overlay.
Dewey Decimal classification system.

```
TR
37              Initial consonant sounds M-Z.   Transparency.
                   3M, 1964.
                   25 mounted transparencies, 10"x10", color.
                Phonics.

                   Included is a packet of printed originals
                from which to make transparencies, with instruc-
                tions on how to make them and how to operate an
                overhead projector.

                PHONETICS/ ser
```

Set of transparencies.
Accession classification system.

The circulation card states the total number of transparencies, with accompanying material. To conserve space on the card the symbol TR may be used for transparencies after the number, e.g., 25 transparencies (or 25TR); w/originals & instructions.

PHYSICAL PROCESSING

Place a label with the call number and ownership information on each transparency, on all accompanying material, and on the outside of box or envelope. An inventory list may be pasted on the outside of the envelope or inside the lid of the box.

Unprotected and/or single transparencies may be placed in an envelope or folder which will accommodate the 12" wide x 10½" high standard transparency mount, labeled, and filed in a box or file cabinet.

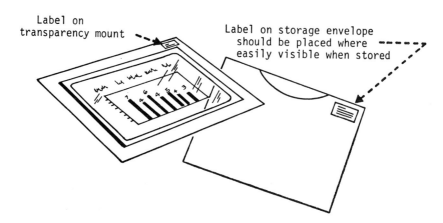

FIGURE 41. TRANSPARENCIES

Manila envelope-stock transparency folders may be procured from Demco.
Learning Resource Products, 3607 Waller Road, Tacoma, Washington, 98443, provides two types of folders made of light weight card stock. One is plain, the other has an opening, or window, which permits viewing of the transparency without removing it from the folder.

SOURCES OF ACQUISITION INFORMATION

Source Directory: Prepared Transparencies. Graflex, Inc., 3750 Monroe Ave., Rochester, N.Y. 14603. $1.00.
A useful quick reference booklet on where transparencies on various subjects and grade levels may be purchased. Request latest edition.

Milton Bradley Co., Dept. TI–1069, Springfield, Mass. 01101.
Produces motion transparencies.

Technamation, Inc., Port Washington, N.Y. 11050.
Produces motion transparencies.

VERTICAL FILE MATERIALS
SYMBOL: VF   COLOR CODE: PINK STRIP

DEFINITION   Vertical file materials are miscellaneous items which are not individually cataloged because of poor physical durability, varied sizes, and short subject treatment. Pamphlets, leaflets, clippings, unmounted pictures printed on light weight paper, are examples.

CATALOGING

A subject card only is made for Vertical File materials. It may refer in general terms to all the materials on the subject to be found in the Vertical File, or specifically to a particular item. The material cataloged in the sample is a pamphlet. Nonprint materials, such as pictures and transparencies (handled as Vertical File resources) are treated in the same manner.

GENERAL REFERENCE SUBJECT CARD

CALL NUMBER   The symbol VF only is used, without any other letters.

SUBJECT HEADING   In capitals, 2nd indention, 2nd line from the top of the card.

MATERIAL IDENTIFICATION AND LOCATION   In main entry position, type a statement which describes the kind of material (general category, or specific type) and where it may be found, e.g., Materials (or, clippings, postcards, pamphlets) on this subject will be found in the Vertical File.

```
        ENGINEERING AS A PROFESSION

VF          Materials on this subject will be found in the
            Vertical File.
```

Vertical File materials.
General reference subject card.

SPECIFIC REFERENCE SUBJECT CARD

This card may be made if the format and content warrant specific identification of the item.

Title main entry is followed by material identification (e.g., Pamphlet), publisher, and date. No collation is given. No tracings are made.

TEACHING AS A PROFESSION

VF   Teaching as a career, by W. H. Burton. Pamphlet. Bellman, 1963.

Vertical File materials. Pamphlet.
Specific reference subject card.

CIRCULATION

If the library policy is to circulate, as a unit, entire folders on a subject, one circulation card is made showing the symbol VF and the subject heading assigned to that folder.

If separate items are charged out a circulation card is made for each, bearing the symbol VF, the subject heading assigned to it, title, and material identification. The provision of a pre-printed form requiring the user to fill in pertinent information is an alternate method for a borrowing record.

```
┌─────────────────────────────────────────────────┐
│ VF                                                │
│       ENGINEERING AS A PROFESSION                 │
│                                                   │
│                                                   │
│                                                   │
├──────────┬──────────────────────┬────────────────┤
│          │                      │                │
├──────────┼──────────────────────┼────────────────┤
│          │                      │                │
├──────────┼──────────────────────┼────────────────┤
│          │                      │                │
└──────────┴──────────────────────┴────────────────┘
```

Circulation card for Vertical File subject folder.

```
┌─────────────────────────────────────────────────┐
│ VF                                                │
│       TEACHING AS A PROFESSION                     │
│          Teaching as a career. Pam-               │
│       phlet.                                       │
│                                                   │
├──────────┬──────────────────────┬────────────────┤
│          │                      │                │
├──────────┼──────────────────────┼────────────────┤
│          │                      │                │
├──────────┼──────────────────────┼────────────────┤
│          │                      │                │
└──────────┴──────────────────────┴────────────────┘
```

Circulation card for individual Vertical File material.

PHYSICAL PROCESSING

On each piece of material stamp ownership, and write VF and subject heading (in capitals) in upper corner.

File in the Vertical File, alphabetically by subject heading, either separately, or in folders or envelopes labeled with appropriate subject headings. If desired, a pocket for the circulation card may be pasted on the inside of the front cover of the folder.

BIBLIOGRAPHY

Gould, Geraldine, and Ithmer C. Wolfe. *How to Organize and Maintain the Library Picture/Pamphlet File.* Dobbs Ferry, N.Y.: Oceana Publications, 1968.

VIDEO TAPES
SYMBOL: MV   COLOR CODE: BLUE

DEFINITION   A magnetic tape which records sound *and* picture from a television source, for playback on television equipment.

With the recognition of the many-faceted educational values of television more and more libraries are acquiring video tape collections. Due to rapid changes in the television art and lack of standardization in equipment for production, playback and transmission, there is presently a confusing variety of tapes and recorders. No tapes should be purchased before definitely ascertaining that they can be played on the equipment available. Those who are responsible for ordering pre-recorded tapes should have information on the tape specifications for their system, and orders should always specify the manufacturer and model number of the playback equipment. The important physical characteristics of tapes which should be checked for compatibility to equipment include:

TAPE WIDTH   Available in 2" (most commonly used in commercial production), 1", ½", ¼".

SPEED   Available in 7½ and 15 inches per second, and in various other speeds such as 4.25, 8.46, 9.6, 12 ips.

REEL SIZES: May vary from 7" to 14".

CATALOGING

COLLATION   Total running time in minutes, or the number of parts or lessons and the running time of each, manufacturer and model number of playback system preceded by the word "for." This information obviates the necessity of stating speed, tape width, and reel size.

NOTES   If applicable, and not already noted in the collation, state the number of parts or lessons.

```
MV
507       Adventures in science experiments.  Video tape.
Ad            Tilden, Calif., Curriculum Center, 1967.
              20 min., b&w., for Ampex VR-6000.    4-6.
              Teaching guide.

              Ten experiments demonstrate basic concepts
          in science.



          SCIENCE- EXPERIMENTS
```

*Video tape.
Dewey Decimal classification system.

```
MV
6500      Our small world.  Video tape.     Planets, 1968.
              15 lessons, 10 min. each, b&w., for Sony PV-
          120U.    4-8.

              Instruction in geography emphasizes relation-
          ships between various parts of the world.



          GEOGRAPHY
```

*Video tape.
Accession classification system.

PHYSICAL PROCESSING

On a label type the manufacturer and model number of the playback equipment to be used and affix it to the center of the reel. Process the same as films.

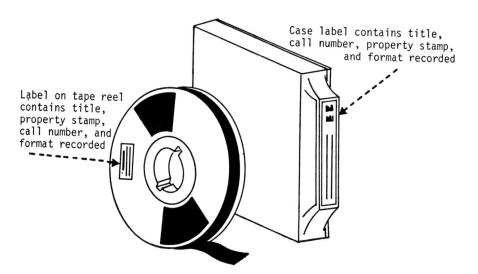

Label on tape reel
contains title,
property stamp,
call number, and
format recorded

Case label contains title,
call number, property stamp,
and format recorded

FIGURE 42. VIDEO TAPE AND CARRYING CASE

BIBLIOGRAPHY

Some information and advertisements appear in various issues of *Audiovisual Instruction*.

Geith, Robert W. "Video Tape Recorders: A Study in Incompatibility," *EPIE Forum* 1, No. 6 (Feb. 1968): 20–21.

REVISION OF LIBRARY OF CONGRESS CARDS

MAIN ENTRY

Where title main entry is used and the Library of Congress main entry is other than by title, erase it or cross it through and type the title main entry on line above. The original L.C. main entry then becomes an added entry. The Library of Congress uses title main entry for films and filmstrips. However, phonorecords may be entered under composer, arranger, or performer, rather than title. Where revision to title main entry becomes so extensive that the card is confusing to read, the use of L.C. cards is not recommended.

OTHER REVISIONS

Suggested Dewey number, subject headings, added entries. Wherever possible, accept L.C. cataloging for these items. Conform to local library cataloging only if L.C. cataloging would create confusion for the user. Delete unnecessary added entries which would be of no interest to the user. Do not revise the body of the L.C. card.

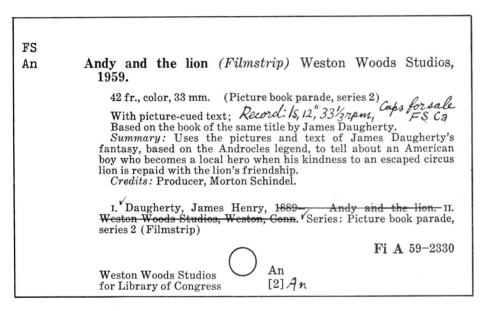

Revised L.C. card.

Fiction.

Filmstrip with accompanying material with a different call number.

FORM 17. REVISION OF LIBRARY OF CONGRESS CARD

FS
539   **Atoms and atomic energy** (*Filmstrip*)   Eye Gate House,
At   1964.

          45 fr., color, 35 mm.   (Fundamentals of science, grade 9, no. 6)

          With teachers manual, *Sound F S 534 So*
          Summary: Explains the relationship of molecules and atoms. De-
scribes the various kinds of atoms and where they are found. Dis-
cusses the elements, including radium and uranium. Points out the
uses of atomic energy.

          1. Atoms——~~Juvenile films.~~   2. ~~Atomic energy—Juvenile films.~~
~~i. Eye Gate House, inc.~~   Series: Fundamentals of science, grade 9
(Filmstrip) ~~no. 6.~~

                                                      Fi A 64–2167

Eye Gate House   ◯ **539**
for Library of Congress   [1½]

Revised L.C. card.

Non-fiction.

Filmstrip with accompanying material with a different call number.

FORM 18. REVISION OF LIBRARY OF CONGRESS CARD

When an insufficient number of L.C. cards is provided, use the L.C. cards
for the public catalog. Type the shelf-list card, deleting unessential information
such as 35mm, annotation.

```
FS
539        Atoms and atomic energy.  Filmstrip.  Eye Gate,
At            1964.
              45 fr., color.  Fundamentals of science,
           grade 9.
              Teachers manual, Sound FS 534 So.




           ATOMS/ ser
```

Revised L.C. card for shelf-list.

If an additional added entry card is needed, eliminate unessential information and rewrite annotation so that a continuation card is not required.

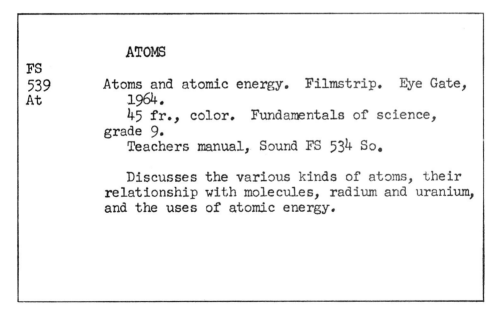

```
              ATOMS
FS
539        Atoms and atomic energy.  Filmstrip.  Eye Gate,
At            1964.
              45 fr., color.  Fundamentals of science,
           grade 9.
              Teachers manual, Sound FS 534 So.

              Discusses the various kinds of atoms, their
           relationship with molecules, radium and uranium,
           and the uses of atomic energy.
```

Revised L.C. card for added entry.

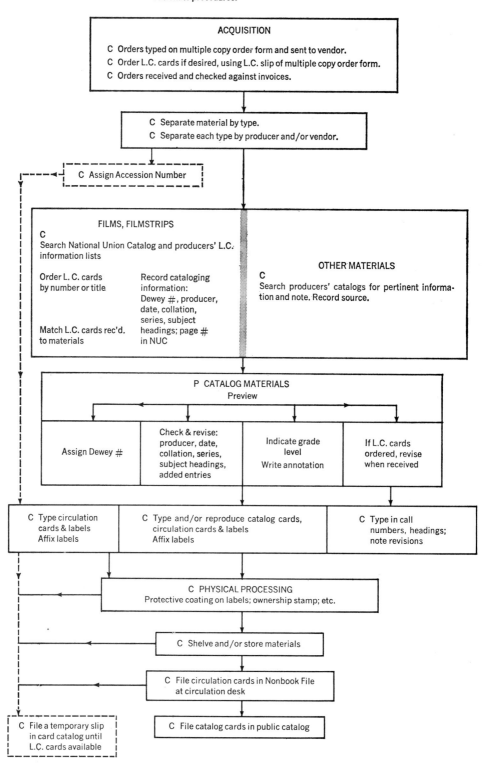

CODE: C—Clerical procedures; P—Professional procedures;
————Alternate procedures.

ACQUISITION

C Orders typed on multiple copy order form and sent to vendor.
C Order L.C. cards if desired, using L.C. slip of multiple copy order form.
C Orders received and checked against invoices.

C Separate material by type.
C Separate each type by producer and/or vendor.

C Assign Accession Number

FILMS, FILMSTRIPS
C
Search National Union Catalog and producers' L.C.
information lists

| Order L. C. cards by number or title | Record cataloging information: Dewey #, producer, date, collation, series, subject headings; page # in NUC |
| Match L.C. cards rec'd. to materials | |

OTHER MATERIALS
C
Search producers' catalogs for pertinent informa-
tion and note. Record source.

P CATALOG MATERIALS
Preview

| Assign Dewey # | Check & revise: producer, date, collation, series, subject headings, added entries | Indicate grade level Write annotation | If L.C. cards ordered, revise when received |

| C Type circulation cards & labels Affix labels | C Type and/or reproduce catalog cards, circulation cards & labels Affix labels | C Type in call numbers, headings; note revisions |

C PHYSICAL PROCESSING
Protective coating on labels; ownership stamp; etc.

C Shelve and/or store materials

C File circulation cards in Nonbook File at circulation desk

C File a temporary slip in card catalog until L.C. cards available

C File catalog cards in public catalog

FIGURE 43. CATALOGING AND PHYSICAL PROCESSING WORK
FLOW CHART

Index